# ROUTE 1

## NEW ENGLAND

### DAN TOBYNE

The Point

Down East Books

# Down East Books

An imprint of Globe Pequot

Distributed by NATIONAL BOOK NETWORK

Copyright © 2017 by Dan Tobyne

Photographs: Dan Tobyne

British Library Cataloguing in Publication Information available

Library of Congress Cataloging-in-Publication Data available

ISBN 978-1-60893-618-2 (hardcover)
ISBN 978-1-60893-619-9 (e-book)

The paper used in this publication meets the minimum requirements of American National Standard for Information Sciences—Permanence of Paper for Printed Library Materials, ANSI/NISO Z39.48-1992.

Printed in the United States of America

"When the Indian trail gets widened, graded, and bridged to a good road, there is a benefactor, there is a missionary, a pacificator, a wealth bringer, a maker of markets, a vent for industry"

— Ralph Waldo Emerson

# CONTENTS

# INTRODUCTION

>>>>You would never try to describe your best friend to someone. You'd probably start with his personality. The same goes for America's greatest roadway. Route 1 is a living, breathing, manifestation of America. It is as much about the people as it is about the place; as much about the buildings, bridges, and monuments, as it is about the view. For a taste of the "lifeblood of America," look no farther than a simple jaunt down U.S. Highway 1. It can be dirty and pristine, fast and interminably slow, poor and affluent. It encompasses all walks of life, and it tells our story.

Route 1 traverses New England for 784 miles, a grand roadway rich in history, natural resources, and people. It's a roadway uniquely

enriched by the people who call the land along this asphalt strip their home. They are the resource that makes the real difference.

Before it was called Route 1, it was known as the Atlantic Highway, replacing the even older designation of the Quebec-Miami International Highway. In the early part of the twentieth century the road also had other names, many harkening back to the days of turnpikes: the Boston Post Road, Newbury Turnpike, and the Norfolk and Bristol Turnpike, to name a few.

In Maine, Route 1 runs along the state's Northern Cap, before entering the beautiful land known as Down East. From the northeast corner of Maine it continues south through the barrens, before entering the southern coastal plain. In New Hampshire it makes a brief appearance for a mere seventeen miles, but brings the traveler to Portsmouth with its rich maritime history.

Entering Massachusetts at Salisbury, the roadway runs a gauntlet of small towns before reaching Boston, the real cradle of liberty. Running farther south, it enters Rhode Island, the birthplace of the industrial revolution in America, before again finding its way to the shore as it meanders through the hamlets of historic Connecticut.

I thought writing this book would be easy because it had a beginning, middle, and end. It wasn't. It was complex, and at times baffling, until I realized what I was trying to communicate was an essence of time and place.

As a photographer, I try to share stories with my pictures. To balance photos and text, I started getting caught up with statistics—this many acres of potatoes, how many pounds of lobsters per state, etc., and that was a mistake.

In the end, I left them out because these numbers didn't capture the life I was witnessing. The other issue I struggled with was, believe it or not, "facts." I found more disputed facts than you could shake a stick at during research for this project. I still can't figure out what town is the birthplace of the American Navy, what group fought the first naval battle of the Revolutionary War, or why the United States Department of Education's Teacher Study Guide says Samuel Slater started the Industrial Revolution in Beverly, Massachusetts.

I hope I have my facts straight and I hope I've given enough information, but my real goal was and is to give you a flavor and a feel for the people and places that make Route 1 a great place for those who want to get out and explore.

Lupines can be spotted along roadways and in fields anyplace in Maine, giving the impression they've probably been there forever, but they aren't native to the state. They are, however, very beautiful and anyone who's tried to plant or replant them will agree, they're often mysterious.

# MAINE

## The Northern Cap—Land of the Acadians

**Fort Kent** • **Frenchville** • **Madawaska** • **Grand Isle** • **Van Buren** •
**Cyr Plantation** • **Conner** • **Caribou** • **Presque Isle**

### FORT KENT

>>>>Route 1's first mile begins at a granite monument in Fort Kent, Maine, located just over the International Bridge connecting Canada and the United States. The monument is new and so is the bridge, prime examples of this epic roadway's restlessness. From the businesses that bloom and fade to its constant repositioning, Route 1 is one of the least sleepy roadways in America.

For many that live in the Fort Kent area the border crossing is more a line between neighborhoods then between nations. When the Saint John River Valley was settled it was one of the last places the Acadian people found to settle as a community, and they planted themselves on both sides of the river.

The Acadian culture in northern Maine has always been built around family values, a dedication to religious beliefs, an enduring work ethic, and a strong sense of community.

#### THE THERIAULT'S

A good example of Acadian strength and perseverance are the Theriault's of Fort Kent. Edmond and Brian are snowshoe makers and ambassadors of Maine's cultural heritage, traveling the

The beginning of the Can-Am Crown International Sled Dog Races at Fort Kent, Maine. Held each year in early March.

The Can-Am Crown International Sled Dog Races are held in early March at Fort Kent. Contestants compete in one of three races; a thirty-mile, one-hundred mile, and the big one, a two-hundred-and-fifty-miler. The largest race is a prequalifying race for mushers and their teams who want to qualify for Alaska's famous Iditarod.

Long before the snowmobile helped people move around, the dogsled performed similar duties. It was used for anything and everything associated with moving things and people from one place to another. Dog sledding—seldom used for work today—is still around. It's now a sport.

The starting line for the Can-Am is in the middle of the street, just beyond the Route 1 mile marker.

Just behind the Can-Am's starting line, nestled in a stand of pines is the Fort Kent Blockhouse. This National

historic landmark located at the confluence of the St. John and Fish rivers is the only remaining section of a fort built to protect U.S interests in the region.

**ABOVE:** A team of sled dogs head off at theCan-Am Crown International Sled Dog Race.

country demonstrating a skill they hope to pass on to others. Brian, Edmond's son, has even written a book on how to make your own set of winter walkers.

I asked Edmond what he did in addition to making shoes for a living (Edmond is 90 years old) and his answer came quickly; *"Whatever we could do, we did"*, and by "we" he meant his family. For the Theriault's and many Acadians, work is almost as important as family and Edmond put it all in perspective; *"It's simple, you work, you are able to help support your family. You are responsible and you feel good about yourself. What's more important than family?"*

**RIGHT:** Today only about 10% of Aroostook County potato stock is available for table consuption. Twenty-five percent of the potatoes grown are sold for seed stock to potato growers around the eastern U.S., 45% are grown for the french fry market, and 20% are used for potato chips. These are Kennebecs, a favorite potato of backyard farmers.

## POTATOES

From Van Buren to Holton, Route 1 runs in a straight line as it passes through vast fields of potatoes and wheat. Potatoes are a primary crop in the region, both for market and as seed potatoes, but also for use in processed foods such as potato chips.

Anyone travelling along Route 1 in Aroostook County will see signs all along the road

# POUTINE

Most Route 1 restaurants along Maine's northern cap serve ethnic comfort food, such as ployes, poutine (gravy and fries smothered with cheese), creton, and an assortment of homemade soups and stews. Creton is a classic Acadian pork spread best served on toast. It's often called a paté, but for those who love it, it's a great substitute for peanut butter.

My grandmother Thibault's recipe for creton;

## INGREDIENTS:

1 pound ground pork,
1 cup milk,
1 onion chopped, garlic,

salt and pepper to taste,
pinch of cloves,
pinch of allspice,
¼ cup of bread crumbs.

Combine the ground pork, milk, onion, and garlic in a saucepan. Season the mixture with salt, pepper, cloves, and allspice. Cook over medium heat for 1 hour, stir in the bread crumbs. Cook for 10 additional minutes. Place in a container, cover and refrigerate.

way advertising potatoes for sale. Five- and ten-pound bags of "reds" or "whites" can be purchased at any of these roadside stands using the honor system. Take a bag and leave the money in the box.

**RIGHT:** Poutine

## AROOSTOOK FARM

Aroostook Farm is a 425-acre research facility located at 59 Houlton Road, Route 1, in Presque Isle. The farm, an extension of the University of Maine, is responsible for the development of new potato varieties, the detection of potato viruses, and the improvement of potato quality. It's been assisting farmers since 1915.

**ABOVE:** The barn dominates the entrance to the 425-acre Aroostook Farm. The farm is part of the University of Maine and does research and development for the potato industry, including the development of new potato varieties.

## ACADIAN VILLAGE

The Acadian Village is operated by the Living Heritage Society of Van Buren and depicts Acadian life through its unique collection of original and reproduction buildings. A tour of the village gives insight into life in Aroostook County from the early days to the twentieth century.

## ACADIAN FESTIVAL

The Acadian Festival is held each year in August in downtown Madawaska. It includes a parade and a reenactment of the first Acadian Landing on the banks of the St. John River near the present day Tante Blanche Museum.

**LEFT TOP:** Most of the buildings on-site were original structures moved to this location and furnished with period items. The Roy House is a low-ceilinged farmhouse built with log construction, and moss for insulation. When weather turned cold it was a common practice to move the farm animals indoors to protect them and to help warm the interior. **LEFT MIDDLE:** One-room schoolhouse. **LEFT BOTTOM:** Acadian Village Country Store and Gift Shop.

## PLOYE FESTIVAL AND MUSKIE DERBY

The Ploye Festival and Muskie Derby are held on the same weekend every August. One of the highlights of the festival is the cooking of the largest ploye, a French Acadian buckwheat pancake. Other events scheduled in Fort Kent during the festival include a ploye eating contest and a craft fair.

The Muskie Festival attracts sportsmen from all over the region angling for part of the $35,000 prize. There are prizes for the largest Muskie and Bass taken from eligible waters. The derby officially opens Friday morning and concludes on Sunday night.

## MUSÉE CULTUREL DU MONT-CARMEL

This former Catholic church, owned by the L'Association culturelle et historique du Mont-Carmel is now a museum exhibiting the religious and cultural life of the Acadian people. The church, with its Baroque belfries and fenestrated façade, is a great example of the historic wooden catholic churches that once existed in the county.

The Musee Cultural du Mont-Carmal with its baroque belfries and trumpeting archangels.

## EAT HERE

Dolly's Restaurant
Robin's Restaurant
Rock's Family Diner
Rosetta's Restaurant
The Swamp Buck

**ABOVE:** The inside of the Musee Culturel du Mont-Carmel church. The church has been converted into a museum displaying Acadian artifacts.

# Potato and Timber Country

Westfield • Mars Hill • Blaine • Bridgewater • Monticello • Littleton • Houlton •
Hodgdon • Cary Plantation • Amity • Orient • Weston • Danforth • Brookfield • Topsfield •
Waite • Indian Township • Princeton • Baileyville • Baring Plantation

## THE PLANETS

Driving along Route 1 in northern Maine you might be surprised to see a number of odd colored spheres sitting on poles along the roadway. The lollipop like objects are part of the University of Maine at Presque Isle's, Maine Solar System Model.

The Maine Solar System Model is located along forty miles of Maine's Route 1 in northern Aroostook County and at a scale of 1:93,000,000 it's the biggest model of our solar system in the world. The center of our solar system, the sun, is a giant yellow ring located at the Northern Maine Museum of Science, and the planets are scattered along the next forty miles of roadway.

**ABOVE:** Jupiter - Part of the Maine Solar System Model

The vista at the Million Dollar View Scenic Byway located in Weston and Danforth.

Jupiter, Uranus, Saturn, and Neptune are scattered in various fields beside the road. Earth sits in a car dealership, and Mars is located on the grounds of the University of Maine. The model was built under the supervision of the university with volunteer help, creating a great opportunity for family and friends to go on a one-of-a-kind planetary scavenger hunt.

## MILLION DOLLAR VIEW

The stretch along Maine's Route 1 from Orient to Danforth is home to the Million Dollar View Scenic Byway, an eight-mile stretch offering spectacular scenic vistas. The byway offers two turn-offs along the Peekaboo Mountain section to view the Chiputnetiook chain of lakes to the east and as far away as Mt. Katahdin to the west. The lakes include East Grand, North, Mud, Spednic, and Palfrey Lakes that run along the international border between New Brunswick and Maine.

Go to the town of Bailyville and you'll experience a piece of living history that's quickly disappearing—a fully functioning pulp mill. In the mid-1900s there were hundreds of pulp and paper mills operating in the Pine Tree state producing a variety of paper products, including tissue, newsprint, corrugated board products, and much more. They were the economic engines that drove Maine's economy. Today there are only a few mills left.

Pulp production has a distinct smell—my friend loves it, and it wasn't uncommon during paper's heyday to smell a mill long before you saw it. To me it always smelled of boiled cabbage, but to those that make their living in the industry, it smelled like money. Take a short drive off Route 1 in Bailyville to see one. You'll be able to experience a fully functioning paper mill with stacks pushing steam into the air, train cars and lumber trucks loaded with Maine hardwood waiting to feed the beast, and the olfactory smell of pulp production hanging in the air.

One of the last remaining paper mills in Maine located in the town of Woodland

## STATE PARKS

For camping and hiking enthusiasts Maine is a prime destination and some of the best campsites in Maine are along Route 1.

### Aroostook State Park

Aroostook State Park was created in 1939 and is Maine's oldest parkland. The park became a reality after local citizens donated 100 acres to the State of Maine. Today, with the state's purchase of additional land, the park encompasses over 800 acres. The park offers camping at thirty wooded sites, as well as canoeing, fishing, and swimming on Echo Lake, and cross-country skiing and hiking on a number of trails, including those on Quaggy Jo Mountain.

## Cobscook Bay State Park

Cobscook Bay State Park is part of the 24,400 acre Moosehorn National Wildlife Refuge. Cobscook Bay State Park consists of almost 900 acres of pristine Downeast parkland along Cobscook Bay. Cobscook in Passamaquoddy means "boiling tides" and accurately describes the high tidal ranges of Maine's northern coastline, sometimes a 30-foot swing. The park includes 106 campsites, a boat launch, sheltered coves, and mudflats. The estuary has strong tides due to its narrowness and the speed of the tides. Cobscook is a great place to view wildlife and is known to have the largest concentration of bald eagles in Maine. More than 200 species of birds inhabit the region. The

The shoreline along Whiting Bay at low tide, part of Cobscook Bay State Park.

park is also part of Maine's Ice Age Trail that follows the landscape of the last great Wisconsinan ice sheet that covered North America 12,000 years ago.

### Lamoine State Park

Lamoine State Park is located on the Mount Desert Narrows and a short drive from Acadia National Park. Activities include camping, hunting, fishing, and sea kayaking. This oceanfront park is a quiet alternative that also offers easy access to Bar Harbor, Mt. Desert Island, and Acadia National Park.

### Camden Hills State Park

Camden Hills State Park is located a few miles north of downtown Camden. It includes Mt. Battie, affording a picture-perfect view of Camden Harbor and Penobscot Bay. The campground has 107 campsites with many amenities, including RV hookups. Mt. Megunticook is the highest of the Camden Hills and offers many opportunities for hiking on a variety of trails. The park extends across the street to the ocean side of Route 1, with additional trails and ocean access. Other activities available include biking, snowmobiling, cross-country skiing, snowshoeing, picnicking, and horseback riding.

# Down East

Calais ● Robbinston ● Perry ● Pembroke ● Dennysville ● Edmunds ● Whiting ● East Machias ● Machias ● Jonesboro ● Columbia Falls ● Harrington ● Cherryfield ● Milbridge ● Steuben ● Gouldsboro ● Sullivan ● Hancock ● Ellsworth ● Orland ● Bucksport ● Stockton Springs ● Searsport ● Belfast ● Northport

The barrens in all their glory.

〉〉〉〉The barrens often feel like a sleepy, quiet, passed-over section of Maine, but this region is far from it. The barrens produce about 100 million pounds of wild blueberries annually, and beginning in late July or early August, thousands of workers flood the region to pick berries.

Two other economic engines in this part of Maine are boatbuilding and wreath making. Three large wreath companies, the Worcester Wreath Company, Wreaths of Maine, and Whitney Wreath make their home in this part of the state. Millions of wreaths are made each year in Maine by families, church groups, and local businesses.

Traditional wreath making in Maine uses balsam fir and is

The Worcester Wreath Company building, one of three large wreath manufacturers in Maine.

considered a renewable and sustainable industry because only the end-portion of the branch, known as the "tip," is used in the making of a Maine wreath.

Boatbuilding happens all over Maine, but in Steuben, the craftsmen of H & H Marine build lobster boats. Anyone driving along this section of Route 1 can't help but spot the boat-like hull molds sitting on the side of the road.

Maine is also home to some of the best boatbuilding schools in America, dedicated to sharpening the skills of the next generation of craftsmen.

**ABOVE::** The St. Croix International Historic Site.

**LEFT:** Red Beach is located near the St. Croix International Historic Site. It's a high concentration of red feldspar that gives the rock its red color. **BELOW:** Downtown Calais.

## CALAIS

Don't miss the St. Croix International Historic Site in Calais. In 1604, French explorer Pierre Dugas established a small outpost on St. Croix Island in an attempt to colonize the land that would eventually become known as l'Acadie (Acadia). Suffering terrible winter conditions, the inhabitants eventually moved to the mainland the following spring and established the settlement of Port-Royal in present-day Nova Scotia. Today St. Croix Island is an International Historic Site and the National Park Service maintains a visitor's center and park at 84 Saint Croix Drive, just off Route 1 in Calais.

# ROBBINSTON

A fish weir is a type of trap for catching fish, usually in a tidal zone near a river or estuary. The concept is simple. Fish swim along an obstruction in the water until they enter an open space that's actually a circular pen. Once in they can't figure out how to get out. Fishermen either net the fish from small boats or wait until the tide goes out to collect their catch. Weirs once dotted New England's tidal landscape, trapping herring, salmon, eels, and whatever else swam in and couldn't get out. They're all but nonexistent today, but for those with a sharp eye, you can still find classic fish weirs in Maine. In South Robbinston there's a small pullout next to a large tidal estuary at the intersection of Route 1 and Katie Lane. Looking east at low tide, you'll see a classic coastal fish weir. The other location is just off Route 1 in Perry. In the 1800s fish weirs were set up at Birch and Gleason's Points, and at East Bay to catch herring for the sardine canneries at Eastport and Perry. There's still one remaining weir located at a little-known state park. Take Shore Road to Gleason Point Road. At the end of Gleason Point Road, you'll find the beach, the fish weir, and great views of Passamaquoddy Bay.

A fish weir used to trap fish. Once they swim into the circular pen they usually can't figure out how to exit. Weirs were once stationed up and down the New England coast.

## WILD BLUEBERRY LAND

Cherryfield might brag that it's the Blueberry capital of the world, but Colombia Falls is home to the biggest and baddest blueberry of all time. Wild Blueberry Land is a large geodesic dome filled with all things blueberry, including blueberry coffee, blueberry ice cream, blueberry fudge—they have it all. Even the bathrooms are blueberry. It's a great place to stop if you're hungry. They have a wonderful selection of home-made pies, candies, and pastries. If you have a little time, you can even play a round of blueberry themed mini-golf.

**ABOVE:** Wild Blueberry Land in Columbia Falls.
**BELOW:** You can pick-your-own at many of the farms in the barrens.

**ABOVE:** This vessel may no longer be fit for catching lobsters, but that's no reason it can't be used to advertise them.

All along Route 1 there are lobster shacks, stands, vans, pounds, shops, buoys, traps, gifts, and anything and everything related to America's favorite crustacean. Maine's rocky coast and cold water are the ideal habitat for lobsters and Maine lobstermen land about 120 million pounds annually from almost 3 million traps scattered along the sea floor. Lobstering is big business and the state has worked hard to protect this valuable resource.

## FORT KNOX

In Prospect is the largest and most complete historic fort in Maine—Fort Knox. Located on the Penobscot River narrows, it was built to protect the region from attack, ostensibly from Great Britain that had harassed and controlled much of the region during the Revolutionary War, and the War of 1812. Although it never saw action it was garrisoned for over 50 years and today this well preserved historic masterpiece is a great place to visit and explore. It's also believed to be haunted.

**RIGHT:** One of the gun (cannon) batteries, at Fort Knox. Opened in 1844, the fort is rumored to be haunted.

## EAT HERE

**Bob's Clam Shack,** Kittery
**Dolly's,** Frenchville
**Flo's,** York
**Maine Diner,** Wells
**Moody's,** Waldoboro
**Red's Eats,** Wiscasset
**Robert's Grille,** Kittery
**Treats,** Wiscasset
**Wasses Hot Dogs,** Rockland

**ABOVE:** An engineering marvel, in 2006 the Penobscot Narrows Bridge replaced the old Wald-Hancock Bridge between Prospect and Verona Island.

## PENOBSCOT NARROWS BRIDGE

Route 1 turns sharply as it exits Bucksport, crossing over the eastern channel of the Penobscot River on its way to Verona Island. However, it doesn't stay long on Verona and as the roadway begins to turn again, two unique structures come into view, one old, the other new. Before 2006 anyone driving back to the mainland on Route 1 would do so over the Waldo-Hancock Bridge. Built in 1931, it was listed as a National Historic Landmark, but over time the elements took their toll and by 2003 the bridge was beyond repair. In 2006, to much fanfare the new 2,120-foot-long, cable-stayed Penobscot Narrows Bridge, complete with two 420-foot obelisk towers and an observatory, replaced the old bridge. The towers are modeled after the Washington Monument and were even built with the same granite quarried from nearby Mount Waldo. The observatory, open to the public from May through October, sits 42 stories above the road deck and offers a spectacular 360-degree view. On a clear day, they say you can see all the way to Mt. Katahdin.

**LEFT:** The view from under the Penobscot Narrows Bridge. This is the view from the entrace to the observatory greeting center.

**ABOVE:** Mainely Pottery shop exhibits and sells the work of many of the state's best potters.

**ABOVE:** Perry's Nut House is a must see for those that find original one-of-a-kind attractions worth visiting.

# BELFAST

## POTTERY CENTRAL

There are many talented potters working in Maine and I'm sure someone has created a Potter's Trail map showing the various locations, but Maine is a big state, and for those without a lot of time for cruising, *Mainely Pottery*, between Searsport and Belfast offers a great alternative. Opened in 1988, the shop, at 181 Searsport Avenue (Route 1) in Belfast, is owned and operated by Jamie Oates and Jeanette Faunce, and features the work of 28 professional potters from around the state, working in various mediums, including: earthenware, porcelain, wood-fired, stoneware, and raku. Jamie Oates' studio is located next to the shop and the public is welcome to watch him work at his craft.

## PERRY'S NUT HOUSE

Perry's Nut House, located at 45 Searsport Avenue in Belfast, is possibly Maine's original roadside attraction. Once the home of a sea captain, it was bought by M.L. Perry for his cigar-making business. Always the entrepreneur, he began buying pecans from Georgia to sell in Maine, and the business did so well Perry's Nut House was born in 1927. He travelled extensively and was

**ABOVE:** Wooden lobsterman greets visitors at the front door of Perry's Nut House.

a fan of the eclectic, often bringing home strange items that he used to decorate his nut house; a stuffed gorilla, coconuts, alligator and python skins. Perry died in 1940 and the property fell into the hands of Joshua Treat III, who continued decorating the shop with diverse objects, including a man-eating clam from the South Pacific.

The nut business and oddball collections continued to grow and the store became a destination for almost everyone visiting the Maine coast. Featuring lots of unique oddities and gifts for sale, Perry's became a one-of-a-kind shopping experience. But under new management in 1997, most of the "décor" was sold at auction and it looked like Perry's might be going out of business. No more home-made fudge, no more gag gifts, and no more international nut collection. However, when the Nut House was sold again in 2004, the new owners began bringing back some of what made the odd-ball shop unique. Today, Perry's Nut House is once again a must-see destination, filled with strange and entertaining stuff, not to mention great fudge.

Commercial Street Visitors
Center in Bath, Maine, home of
General Dynamics' Bath Iron
Works (BIW), and the Maine
Maritime Museum.

# Mid-Coast Maine

Lincolnville ● Camden ● Rockport ● Rockland ● Thomaston ● Warren ● Waldoboro ● Nobleboro

● Newcastle ● Damariscotta ● Edgecomb ● Wiscasset ● Woolrich ● Bath ● West Bath

〉〉〉〉 Maine's mid-coast is a busy tourist zone with a flood of cars and buses arriving daily. Camden and Wiscasset, two quintessential coastal towns, overflow with visitors during the summer months and have some of the biggest traffic jams you'll ever see. Wiscasset has studied alternatives to roadway design and parking in an attempt to ease the gridlock, including a Route 1 bypass, but at last check, the town had voted down the rerouting scheme and was headed back to the drawing board to come up with an alternative plan. For most of the other mid-coast towns, Route 1 glances past town centers and traffic moves somewhat easier.

Lincolnville Beach

## CAMDEN

Camden was once known for manufacturing and boatbuilding but today it's all about shopping and sailing. It is still one of those rare towns with almost everything concentrated downtown, making it one of the most walkable mid-coast shopping locations you're going to find. It's also home to Maine's resurrected sailing fleet. Schooners, of all sizes—including three that are designated National Historic Landmarks—are available for trips along the coast from half-day sails to week-long excursions. A short walk to the town dock located just behind Main Street feels like a step back in time with the fleet neatly arranged in the quaint harbor.

Camden is a year-round destination. The town hosts one of the great events of the winter season, the United States National Toboggan Championships. Every February teams from all over the east coast gather to compete on the mountain. The completion is open to all, and the atmosphere is usually electric. It's a party in the woods complete with music, bonfire, food, and a giant toboggan chute.

Camden is also home to Mt. Battie, one of only two places along the Maine coast where the mountains meet the sea.

ABOVE Schooners in Camden Harbor.
BELOW Autumn view of Camden from Mt. Battie.

**ABOVE:** The famous Reny's.

Just beyond Camden's busy downtown is a small shopping plaza with a Reny's Department Store, and I never pass by without stopping in. They don't sell online so the only way to find some of their great deals is to stop in and explore. The first store was opened in 1949 by Robert Reny, and his philosophy has helped his business grow to seventeen stores, many located along Route 1 in places like Camden, Belfast, Ellsworth, and Saco. The motto of this family-owned business is: *"Make great buys of quality merchandise and pass these incredible values along at the lowest possible price to our customers."*

They sell quality merchandise including; Carhartt, Woolrich, Chippewa, and Timberland, with the belief that you can find everything you need at Reny's. If you spend any time at all in Maine, you're bound to hear someone say. "Hey, check this out. I bought it at Reny's."

## ROCKLAND

### FARNSWORTH ART MUSEUM

The Farnsworth is an internationally recognized museum located in Rockland. The museum, with 20,000 square feet of gallery space, is home to the works of the Wyeth's—N.C., Andrew, and Jamie, an artist family that was very successful in capturing iconic Maine. The museum also owns the Olson House, made famous by Andrew Wyeth's paintings of the house, and the people who lived there—Alvaro Olson and his sister Christina. His 1949 painting, *Christina's World*, is probably his most recognizable painting of that era.

**BELOW:** The Eat sculpture sits on the roof of the Farnsworth Museum's Museum Store. It's the work of Robert Indiana and was commissioned for the 1964 World's Fair.

**RIGHT:** Rockland's window art portrayed in this picture shows how the town has become a destination spot for tourists. The North Atlantic Blues Festival and the Maine Lobster Festival draw large crowds. There are a variety of other celebrations throughout the year, including the Maine Boats, Homes and Harbors Show in late summer, and the Rockland Festival of Lights in November.

## SIDE TRIP TO THE OLSON HOUSE

From 1939 to 1968, Andrew Wyeth sketched and painted the Olson Farm in Cushing. His most recognized painting; *Christina's World* hangs in New York City's Museum of Modern Art and is one of the most recognizable paintings of the twentieth century. The farm was gifted to the Farnsworth Art Museum in 1991 and was designated a National Historic Landmark in 2011.

**ABOVE:** The Olson Farm in Cushing, Maine was one of Andrew Wyeth's favorite locations to sketch and paint. Starting in 1939, Wyeth created over 300 illustrations of the farm and it's inhabitants; Christina Olson and her brother Alvaro.

# WISCASSET

Wiscasset has a strong shipbuilding history and, located ten miles up the Sheepscot River, was once a major port offering protection from the dangerous seas. The coming of the railroad brought an end to all of that and today the town is a tourist destination harboring unique shops and restaurants, including the world-famous Red's Eats. It's also famous for being home to one of the biggest Route 1 traffic jams in Maine during the summer tourist season, with traffic backing up in both directions for miles.

Regardless of traffic, Wiscasset is a great place to visit. It boasts a picture-perfect historic downtown and fantastic shopping and restaurant options, including one of my favorites; Stacy Linehan's shop, Treats, located at 80 Main Street. In Stacy's words, it's "a place to gather, eat, and share."

**BELOW:** Downtown Wiscasset has been designated a National Historic District. Of special note is the Nickels-Sortwell House on Main Street and Castle Tucker a few blocks away. Red's Eats, the most publicized lobster-roll seller in Maine, is located at the bottom of the hill. There are a number of antique shops sprinkled downtown, as well as the always interesting Wiscasset General Store.

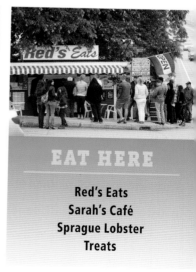

## EAT HERE

**Red's Eats**
**Sarah's Café**
**Sprague Lobster**
**Treats**

**LEFT:** The newest destroyer in the Navy is the Zumwalt class. Built at Bath Iron Works, it is also the largest destroyer ever built, coming in at 600 feet in length. The distinctly sci-fi look of the ship gives it some stealth capability, reducing its radar signature and making it harder to detect.

# BATH

## BATH IRON WORKS

Maine, with more than 3,400 miles of shoreline and five major river systems has a strong boat-building heritage that continues today.

Bath is an especially interesting location to explore boatbuilding. Driving south off the bridge that spans the Kennebec you can't help but notice the giant cranes of the Bath Iron Works shipyard. The Yard, which today specializes in building warships, incorporated in 1884 and the first BIW ship built for the Navy was the iron gunboat *Machias*. The shipyard has constructed many of the Navy's destroyers, frigates, cruisers, and battleships, and the quality of the work has earned them the slogan *"Bath-built is best-built."* The tradition lives on today. They are currently building the Navy's newest destroyer, the stealthy Zumwalt Class. BIW trolley tours are available through the Maine Maritime Museum located just down the street at 243 Washington Street.

Why do people like to go antiquing? Maybe because it feels like a treasure hunt, or they hope to find some long-lost item they had as a youth. On the other hand, maybe they want to purchase something different than the assembly line items found in most stores—perhaps an old style lobster pot. Whatever the reason, thousands of people travel up and down the New England coast rooting and rummaging through piles of discarded treasures looking for something to make a connection with, and Maine is still one of those places where you can find a bargain. My general rule of thumb for treasure hunting along Route 1 is: Northern Maine and Down East for junktiquing, and Southern Maine for antiquing, but like anything else, there are always exceptions to the rule.

## FLEA MARKETS

**Cabot Mills Flea Market,** Brunswick

**Cascade Flea Market,** Saco

**Hobby Horse Flea Market,** Searsport

**Montsweag Flea Market,** Woolwich

**Raceabout Market,** Ellsworth

**Southern Maine Indoor Flea Market,** Scarborough

**LEFT:** Many antique shops are orderly and inventoried and the shop owner knows the value of the items for sale, but sometimes the shops often considered "junk" shops are where you can find the real treasures at the best prices. You just need to know what you're looking for.

# Southern Maine

Brunswick ◦ Freeport ◦ Yarmouth ◦ Cumberland ◦ Falmouth ◦ Portland ◦

South Portland ◦ Scarborough ◦ Saco ◦ Biddeford ◦ Arundel ◦ Kennebunk ◦ Wells ◦

Ogunquit ◦ York ◦ Kittery

## BRUNSWICK

>>>> Its neighbor Freeport often overshadows Brunswick as travelers anxiously anticipate legendary L.L. Bean and the other shops just down the road. However, for those willing to stop and linger, visiting Brunswick can be richly rewarding.

### FAT BOY DRIVE-IN AND NEW BEET MARKET

If you're hungry and looking for something a little different, check out the Fat Boy Drive-In, located at 111 Bath Road. Fat Boy

Brunswick

Maine State Music Theatre
Pejepscot Museum
Bowdoin College  Museum of Art
Peary-MacMillan Arctic Museum
Bowdoin International Music Festival
The Theater Project
Skolfield-Whittier House
Joshua Chamberlain Museum

has been around since 1955. There are a few seats inside but the best way to experience this flashback eatery is by sitting in your car. Flashing your car lights will get someone to take your order and bring it out to the car when ready. The food is cooked to order and the menu has old-time favorites, such as lobster cakes, real onion rings, grilled cheese and fried egg sandwiches, and frappes with real milk and ice cream. For a real treat visit Fat Boy during one of their Sock Hop events, complete with dancing contests, vintage cars, and fifties music. You can't beat it.

If fifties comfort food isn't your thing, go down the road to the New Beet Market for breakfast or lunch at 25 Burbank Street. Their food ingredients are locally sourced and the sandwiches and salads are made to order. Try my favorite, the Orion: egg, cheese, and thick cut Maine bacon on a Hootenanny English muffin. If you finish with a cold-brew coffee, you might never leave.

**ABOVE:** Fat Boy in Bruswick, Maine, is a summer favorite.

## THE JOSHUA L. CHAMBERLAIN MUSEUM

**ABOVE:** While sitting in this church Harriet Beecher Stowe came up with the idea for *Uncle Tom's Cabin.*

You may have heard about the 20th Maine Volunteers and their heroic stand at Little Round Top during the Battle of Gettysburg under the command of Colonel Joshua Chamberlain. Chamberlain, who was a professor and later president of Bowdoin College, volunteered for the army, retiring as a general in 1865. He went on to serve four terms as governor of Maine. Chamberlain died in 1914 and his houset 226 Main Street is now a museum. Interestingly, the house was also once the home of Henry Wadsworth Longfellow.

Just across the street from the Chamberlain house is the First Parish Church, nicknamed Uncle Tom's Church. While sitting in a pew listening to her husband preach, Harriet Beecher Stowe got the spark to write *Uncle Tom's Cabin.*

**RIGHT:** The Joshua L. Chamberlain Museum is located in Brunswick and today operated by the Pejepscot Historical Society. Joshua Chamberlain was President of Bowdoin College and served as the Governor of Maine, but he is probably best remembered for his defense of Little Round Top during the Battle of Gettysburg. The Greek Revival house was also home to Henry Wadsworth Longfellow when he taught at Bowdoin.

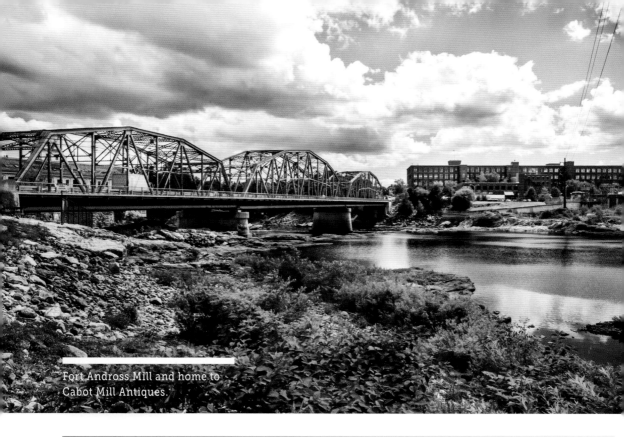

Fort Andross Mill and home to Cabot Mill Antiques.

## MORE BRUNSWICK FUN

Located at the falls of the Androscoggin River, is the Brunswick Hydro Station. The viewing room allows visitors in early summer to watch various fish species, including herring and salmon, make the upriver migration.

Near the hydro station is the old Fort Andross Mill at 14 Maine Street. It is home to Cabot Mill Antiques, a collaborative of some 150 antique dealers all selling their wares in the 16,000 square foot area.

# FREEPORT

With strong historic preservation regulations, much of Freeport's downtown has retained its old world charm. You would never know with a quick glance that there's a McDonald's or Starbucks on Main Street.

In 1911, when a young Leon Leonwood Bean began tinkering with a new idea for a hunting boot, Freeport was just another sleepy coastal town with only 2,000 residents. Today, over one hundred years later, the population has only grown to 8,000, but the town is anything but sleepy.

L.L.'s business quickly outgrew his brother's basement, becoming one of the most successful family-owned retail businesses in the world; and, like a giant magnet, its success has allowed a legion of other brands to find a home in town.

Bean founded his business on a few basic principles—sell well built and tested products,

**BELOW:** Main Street in Freeport with its biggest draw, the LL Bean Main store. Freeport is also home to a large number of other outlet stores, all drawn to this small town because of the success of Freeport's main attraction, LL Bean.

and guarantee satisfaction or give the customer their money back. These values, along with L.L.'s engaging personality and wise marketing skills are the foundation for the company's global success.

## THE IDYLL MOTOR COURT

The Idyll Motor Court has been in business for over 80 years and is still operated by the same family, the Marstaller's, and with the same philosophy, proudly hung in each cabin:

*"To All Who Travel on Life's Road of Pleasure and Pain*
*You who stop here should forget your troubles and griefs, your feuds and hates.*
*Think of the trees here. They have looked skyward for one hundred and fifty years—in sunshine, hail, snow, wind rain, thunderstorms, heat, and cold. It was that combination of these elements, that made them grow. Hard knocks, hard luck, pain and tears are like the storms.*
*May your stay at the Maine Idyll be as a day of sunshine—new courage, friendship, and hope."*

~Ernest Marstaller

The vintage charm of a bygone era combined with modern conveniences makes the Idyll Motor Court the obvious choice for those wanting a slower, calmer pace. Cabins have kitchen facilities, most have fireplaces, and some are handicap accessible. Each cabin is unique but one is unlike any other.

## THE BIG INDIAN

On Route 1 just south of Freeport you can't miss The Big Indian. He was commissioned by Julien Leslie, who wanted something special to catch the eye of people passing by his Casco Bay Trading Post. The statue was built by Rodman Shutt of Pennsylvania, who created the 30-foot,

**ABOVE LEFT:** The motor court is a throwback to the days when traveling the countryside by car was a true adventure, and places like the Idyll were a welcome oasis in a motorist's road trip adventure.

**ABOVE:** Cottage 18, known as "One Maine Pine." It lacks the white clapboard look of the Idyll Court with a stained and decidedly rustic appearance. It was constructed using the lumber from only one Maine pine tree.

1,500 pound Indian replete with full headdress and stern expression. The statue has always attracted attention, even from wannabees who at times have shot their own arrows at the gentle giant. The trading post closed in 1989 but The Big Indian still stands today, looking south as if scanning the roadway for new customers.

## WELLS

Don't be surprised while passing through Wells if you see a strange compilation of eclectic buildings scattered around an open field with a small sign saying; *Closed for Renovations*. This is the Johnson Hall Museum, the brainchild of Bill Johnson. He was an avid collector of all things Americana.  Among his treasures include an identical copy in fiberglass of the copper teapot hanging at City Hall Plaza in Boston (it was made for the movie, *The Brink's Robbery*),

**ABOVE:** The Big Indian sits by the side of the road, looking south, possibly trying to spot new customers.

**RIGHT:** One of the eclectic buildings at the Johnson Museum in Wells.

a Howard Johnson weathervane he salvaged from the HoJo's in Cambridge, Massachusetts, before its demolition, and a Maine road sign with a misspelled word. The train depot is listed on the Federal Register of Historic Places. If the closed for renovations sign ever comes down, Bill's place is a must-see event.

## DOUGHNUTS OR DONUTS

Ever since reading Robert McCloskey's book about Homer Price and the doughnut machine I've been a fan of doughnuts, or as we often spell it in New England, "donuts." Rockport, Maine, has claimed to be the birthplace of the man who invented the hole in the doughnut. He made holes in his pasties and hung them on his ship's wheel, so he could eat and sail at the same time. They even erected a plaque in his honor. Now, a plaque doesn't make a statement true, but if it helps prove our case about New England having the best doughnuts in the world, we'll acknowledge Rockport's claim. The most important mission for doughnut lovers is finding the real ones in a sea of imposters.

Real doughnut shops are getting harder to find, so we've included a list of some of the best locations, and I'll confess without shame, that two of the shops aren't on Route 1, but close enough, and good enough, to be included.

**ABOVE:** Captain Hanson Gregory of Rockport, Maine, invented the hole in the doughnut in 1847.

**ABOVE:** Route 1 has some great doughnut shops.

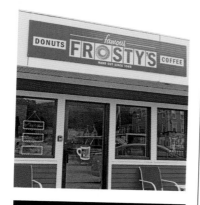

ABOVE: Frosty's donut shop along the donut trail. This one is located in Bath.

ABOVE: The Holy Donut in Portland is famous for its potato donuts.

### Congdon's Doughnuts, Wells

Congdon's has been in business since 1945 and has expanded over the years to include a restaurant, but as always, the mainstay at Congdon's is the doughnuts. They moved around in the early days, settling into their present location in 1955. Today the business is known as Congdon's Family Restaurant and Bakery, but doughnuts are still the biggest attraction. Maple Cream and Chocolate Raised win the day.

### Frosty's Donuts, Brunswick, Freeport, Bath

Frosty's has three locations, with the home store being in Brunswick. We've made an exception for this one. The doughnuts are made in Brunswick and brought to the other stores, and with one owner we consider this store a true doughnut shop. The great thing about this shop is their hours—they open at 4:00 am.

### Holy Donut, Portland

The Holy Donut has two locations, but the one we prefer is closest to Route 1 and their original location at 194 Park Avenue. There is usually a line on weekends that runs down the street. The not-so-secret ingredient in their rounders is mashed Maine potatoes, making them uniquely moist and flavorful. Each morning begins with about twenty flavors and when they're gone, the store closes. We stop and buy a dozen of these whenever we're within striking distance: Dark Chocolate Sea Salt, Maple, and Maple Bacon.

## KITTERY

Route 1 in Kittery is home to a huge sprawl of retail outlets, but the biggest attraction along this shopping gauntlet isn't an outlet at all, but the Kittery Trading Post. It's a family owned operation and has been in business under the Adams family since 1938, catering to hunters and anglers heading north for adventure. Before the multiple traffic lights, turning lanes, and acres of asphalt, the Trading Post occupied its spot with the unspoken message; if you forgot it, we have it. Today it's more of an anchor for the rest of the retail menagerie spread across both sides of the roadway, and for many it's also an acceptable substitute for those not wanting to travel to Freeport to shop at that other outdoor megastore.

**ABOVE:** The Kittery Trading Post

### THE TALE OF TWO BOB'S

In the middle of all this asphalt jungle is an oasis of culinary delight. Sitting diagonally across from each other just north of the Kittery Trading Post is Bob's Clam Hut on the southbound side, and Robert's Maine Grille on the northbound. The Clam Hut has been around since 1956; Robert's not so long, opening their doors in 2006. Both, however, are exceptional

experiences. If you have a hankering for fried clams, fish and chips, or other classic fried dishes, the Clam Hut is the place—their tartar sauce makes all the difference. If you'd rather sit inside and have great farm fair or seafood, head over to Robert's Maine Grille. Once you've

**LEFT:** Bobs Clam Hut. **BELOW:** Robert's Grille in Kittery.

been to both, it won't be hard to decide which one to go to. When we're tired from all the shopping we head to Robert's. When we get pumped up for fried food its over to Bob's we go. Either way, life is good.

## GOOD TO-GO

Speaking of good. When we head out into the wilds of New England these days we always bring some Good To-Go lightweight dehydrated gourmet meals. Jennifer and David, the owners, have set the goal to "elevate your expectations of what trail food can taste like . . . to take a break from whatever adventure you're on, sit down, take a bite, and say, 'Wow!'"

If you're heading up north for an adventure in the great outdoors, you can stop in at the Kittery Trading Post and pick up some of these dehydrated delights, or drive up the road a mile or so, and stop in to the Good To-Go office. As they say on their website; *"Just look for the yellow cape house and the curly haired dog!"* My favorite is the Thai Curry.

**LEFT:** Good To-Go dehydrated gourmet meals for the back-country. You can visit them at 484 U.S. Route 1 in Kittery—just look for the yellow house with the red sign—or head down to the Kittery Trading Post and pick up some packs for your next camping trip.

# SOUTHERN MAINE ANTIQUES

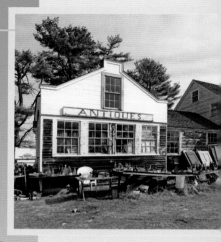

**Antiques U S A**, Arundel

**Armada Antiques & Collectibles**, Kennebunk

**Arundel Antiques**, Arundel

**Barnfull Antiques and Curiosities**, Saco

**Bell Farm Antiques**, York

**Betsey Telford's-Goodwin's Rocky Mountain Antique Quilts**, York

**Bulfinch Antiques**, Kennebunk

**Carriage House Antiques & Estate Sales**, Cape Neddick

**Cattail Farm Antiques, LLC**, Wells

**Chinchillas Antiques**, Kittery Point

**Columbary House Antiques**, Cape Neddick

**Goosefare Antiques**, Wells

**Cranberry Hill Custom Lighting and Antiques**, Cape Neddick

**Hidden Treasures Antiques & Collectibles**, York

**Hooligan's Antiques**, Wells

**Hutchins' Antiques Etc.**, Ogunquit

**J & J Antiques**, Biddeford

**MacDougall-Gionet Antiques & Associates**, Wells

**Noel's Antiques & Collectables**, Wells

**Old House Parts Co**, Kennebunk

**R Jorgensen Antiques**, Wells

**Reed's Antiques & Collectibles**, Wells

**Smith-Zukas Antiques**, Wells

**The Farm Antiques**, Wells

**The York Antiques Gallery**, York

**Victorian Lighting Inc**, Kennebunk

**Wells General Store Antiques**, Wells

Now a state park, Fort McClary was established in 1808 at Kittery Point to provide coastal protection and to prevent invading navies from sailing up the Piscataqua River.

**ABOVE:** Along the waterway in Portsmouth. **RIGHT:** The Memorial Bridge crosses the Piscataqua River between Kittery, Maine, and Portsmouth, New Hampshire.

# NEW HAMPSHIRE

Portsmouth • North Hampton • Hampton • Hampton Falls • Seabrook

>>>>Route 1 runs for a mere seventeen miles through New Hampshire, the shortest distance of all the eastern states, but packs a lot into a small amount of space.

The roadway enters New Hampshire at the once rough-and-tumble seaport city of Portsmouth, now a gentrified tourist destination with a flood of restaurants, shopping venues, and historic sites. Portsmouth is also home to a Route 1 Bypass, a Route 1A and 1B. Beyond Portsmouth the road is more of an eclectic mix of commercial sprawl scattered along the route. Anyone wishing to travel a more picturesque route might want to travel a short distance down 1A. This is the shore route beyond Portsmouth that contains most of the scenic vistas, beaches, and historic sites. There are many gems along all three routes waiting to be discovered.

## PORTSMOUTH

Portsmouth is located along the banks of the Piscataqua River and may be best recognized for its naval heritage, including the Portsmouth Naval Shipyard with its famous prison. The prison is now closed, however, and the shipyard is actually located in Maine, on Seavey Island in Kittery. But for all that, Portsmouth is still connected to the sea with an active deepwater port, a rich historic district that includes the home of John Paul Jones, as well as shipbuilder Richard Jackson's house, the state's oldest structure.

## THE *ALBACORE*

Portsmouth is also home to the USS *Albacore*, a submarine built at the Portsmouth Naval Shipyard and commissioned in 1953. It was built for research experiments around hull design.

**ABOVE:** The USS *Albacore* National Historic Landmark

The Albacore was designed for speed and maneuverability for training submarine hunter- killer crews, and it did so well during test trials that it changed the Navy's mind about hull design. Today's modern American submarines all use the *Albacore*'s basic design. The submarine is now a National Historic Landmark, and is open to the public at Albcore Park in Portsmouth.

## STRAWBERRY BANKE

Sitting on Route 1 just over the bridge from Kittery is Strawberry Banke, the site of Portsmouth's original settlement and now a museum site. The museum recreates what life was like during the early days of America.

**RIGHT:** Ten-acre Strawberry Banke is a living history museum in which visitors can immerse themselves in the past.

**ABOVE:** Strawberry Banke is one of the oldest settlements in New Hampshire and the oldest neighborhood in Portsmouth, dating back to 1630. Noticing an abundance of berry-bearing plants in the area, Captain Walter Neale named his new settlement Strawberry Banke. Today this 10-acre historic neighborhood is a living example of early America, and its transition from a seventeenth century settlement to a 1950s neighborhood.

## PRESCOTT PARK

Along the harbor Prescott Park offers wonderful views of the Piscataqua River, the Portsmouth Naval Yard, and other sections of Portsmouth proper. It is comprised of lawns, gardens, ocean walkways, piers, and docking space. The park was gifted to the city by two sisters, Mary and Josie Prescott, who spent their inheritance buying property along the river to create a garden park for the city. One of the park's highlights is its formal garden.

**LEFT:** Prescott Park is a beautiful ten-acre park that runs along the Portsmouth waterfront. The park hosts a wonderful and packed formal garden, that includes; walkways, sculptures, fountains, and sitting areas. The park is also home to an outdoor theater, common gardens, docking facilities, and a waterfront walkway.

## THE GUNDALOW COMPANY

Across the street from Prescott Park, at 60 Marcy Street, is the Gundalow Company. A gundalow is a historic, flat-bottomed, shallow draft boat—a barge really, that was used to move cargo around in the rivers and estuaries. Most gundalows relied on the tides and river currents to move around, but it was not uncommon for some to have a sail for additional steerage as they moved up and down the river, or on and off the salt marshes if they were harvesting salt hay.

The Gundalow Company was formed in 2002 and in 2011, using drawings from the Smithsonian, they built a gundalow they named *Piscataqua*, continuing the legacy of this unique craft by offering private charters and educational and public sails.

## THE BLACK HERITAGE TRAIL

The Black Heritage Trail is a walking tour focusing on the contributions of African-Americans

**ABOVE:** The Gundalow Company

**ABOVE:** Part of the Black Heritage Trail

to the history of Portsmouth. It also includes information regarding safe houses and Underground Railroad sites during the time of slavery. The tour is walkable and you can explore the sites on your own or take a guided tour offered at various times during the day.

## THE ANTIQUARIAN BOOKSTORE

The Antiquarian Bookstore in Portsmouth has the largest collection of out-of-print and rare book in New Hampshire. They also have a huge inventory of magazines, art, and comic books. They boast more than 250,000 books.

## THE JOHN PAUL JONES HOUSE

Just around the corner from Route 1 on Middle Street stands the John Paul Jones House. John Paul Jones was the first Captain of the Continental Navy and for a time from 1781 to 1782 lived at 43 Middle Street. He was there to oversee the construction of the 74-gun frigate *America*, being built by John Langdon's shipyard across the way in Kittery, Maine. The three-story gambrel house was built in 1758 by an accomplished African-American builder named Hopestill Cheswell. The house is on the National Register of Historic Place and although Jones only lived there for two years, it's the only remaining structure in America with ties to him. This fine example of Georgian architecture is open to the public daily from May to October.

**ABOVE:** John Paul Jones House.

Other historic structures in downtown Portsmouth worth a visit include:

## Jackson House, 1664

The oldest surviving wood frame house in New Hampshire.

## Warner House, 1716

One of the oldest brick mansions in the United States located in an urban setting.

## Tobias Lear House, 1740

Once visited by George Washington, the house at 89 Hunking Street is the birthplace of Tobias Lear V, a confidant and secretary of President Washington.

## Wentworth-Coolidge Mansion, 1750

Benning Wentworth, New Hampshire's first royal governor, lived here from 1752 to 1770. The Coolidge family came in 1886, eventually donating the site to the state in 1954.

## Wentworth Gardner House, 1760

This waterfront mansion, built by Mark Hunking Wentworth as a wedding present for his son, is renowned for its splendid Georgian architecture and ornate carvings. Its spacious eighteenth-century kitchen has a rare fan-driven chimney meat roaster. Arthur Nutting, famous for his landscape photographs of New England, once owned the house.

## Moffatt-Ladd House, 1763

The house was once the home of William Whipple,

**ABOVE AND RIGHT:** Historic building along the water in Portsmouth.

Revolutionary War general and signer of the Declaration of Independence. Of interest to many is the large horse chestnut tree on the property. Whipple planted the tree from a seed he brought back from Philadelphia in 1776.

## Governor John Langdon House, 1784

Home of three-term governor of New Hampshire, shipbuilder and merchant, John Langdon, this house is an example of the wealth of Portsmouth when mercantile business flourished.

## Rundlet-May House, 1807

The Rundlet-May House is great example of a multi-generational home that still has much of its original interior furnishings.

# NORTH HAMPTON AND HAMPTON

## MINI-GOLF

I always thought mini-golf was a game for kids until I met up with the United States Pro Mini-Golf Association, the USPMGA, where the best of the best play for the U.S. Team in International competition. Yes, there's a Mini-Golf Team USA that represents the United States in organized competition, overseen by the World Mini-Golf Sports Federation (WMSF). They expect to be in the Olympics someday.

Eight or thirty-eight, age doesn't matter. Mini-golf isn't a children's game, it's a family game.

**ABOVE:** Hampton **BELOW:** Captain's Cove Mini-Golf

Hampton is home to Captain's Cove, a mini-golf course with a New England flair, complete with sunken boat, water-fall, and trick shots galore. It's the perfect place to go with family or friends.

**ABOVE:** The Old Methodist Meeting House in Seabrook.

## SEABROOK

Travelling south Route 1 passes through the town of Seabrook, although you might not know it's a town at all. You might struggle to find the town center until you spot the large white clapboarded church—the Old Methodist Meeting House sitting along a block that includes the town offices and the historic Boyd School. The school is now a museum open to the public, and the church is a vacant building.

This small town is home to the Seabrook Nuclear Power Plant. The plant is located in the marsh, a cold gray hulking mass of concrete with its domed reactor chamber rising out of the salt hay and seagrass. The company that owns the plant has built the Science and Nature Center at Seabrook Station, including a mile of nature trails and educational information on nuclear energy.

## THROWBACK BREWERY

The Throwback Brewery in North Hampton is unlike any micro-brewery I know. Situated on the historic 1860 Hobbs Farm, they brew up some unique beers with equally unique names like Fat Alberta Imperial Stout, Hog Happy Hefeweizen, and Maple Kissed Wheat Porter, to name a few. They use the word *terroir* to explain the philosophy behind their craft drinks. Terroir means "sense of place" and is used to describe the process of producing special wines using local grapes that, when combined with special weather conditions, soil characteristics, and geography, produces a product with a distinct flavor. Throwback Brewery is attempting to live up to the essence of terroir with beer—they like to call it "beer-oir," and seem to be very successful at it. In addition to the brewery in the old sheep barn, they also have a restaurant.

**ABOVE:** The Throwback Brewery in North Hampton. **RIGHT:** The Old Salt Restaurant in Hampton.

### The Oar House

Located in the Old Harbor section of Portsmouth in an old grain and molasses warehouse.

### Old Ferry Landing

The Landing is located at the old ferry landing that once facilitated transportation to and from Kittery, Maine.

### River House Restaurant

Great views and the best chowder in Portsmouth. Won Best Chowder award three years running at the Prescott Park Chowder Festival.

### The Old Salt Restaurant

Historic inn and restaurant with New England traditional fare. This is the restaurant you'd take your parents or grandparents to.

### The Throwback Brewery

Food made from scratch with fresh local ingredients.

Newburyport Harbor as seen from Salisbury.

# MASSACHUSETTS

Salisbury • Newburyport • Rowley • Topsfield • Danvers • Peabody • Lynnfield • Saugus • Malden • Revere • Chelsea • Boston • Canton • Westwood • Norwood • Sharon • Walpole • Foxborough • Wrentham • Plainville • North Attleborough • Attleboro

>>>>Route 1 enters Massachusetts at the town of Salisbury, but you would hardly know you've changed states until you reach the bridge over the Merrimack River at Newburyport. Historic Newburyport was once a shipbuilding and commercial shipping port. It sits along the Merrimac River and has a wonderfully restored downtown area. Route 1 leaves Newburyport, the state's smallest city along the old Newburyport Turnpike, passing through New England's Great Salt Marsh on its way to Topsfield (home of the oldest fair in America), and Danvers (the site of the Salem Witch-hunt of 1692). Farther south the roadway enters Boston, one of the most historic cities on the East Coast. The road continues along a more rural section of Route 1, including Foxborough, home of the New England Patriots and the sports mecca known as Patriot Place.

## SALISBURY

### ONE ROOM SCHOOLHOUSE

On the triangle of land in the center of town you'll find the Salisbury Public Library, a fairly new building of contemporary design. But the

**ABOVE:** The two-door outhouse at the Pike School.

real treasure sits next to the library, a restored one-room school house. The Pike School was built in 1882, and served grades 1 through 3 until 1917 when it was converted to a fire station. After serving as a fire station for sixty years, the Salisbury Historical Society restored the building to its original design, right down to the two-door outhouse located at the back of the building. Much of the original school was still intact and Society members received period-specific donations to finish the restoration.

## NEWBURYPORT

**ABOVE:** The Essex County Superior Courthouse—one of the oldest active courthouses in the nation.

Newburyport's Essex County Superior Courthouse, located at 145 High Street shouldn't be missed. It sits on the Bartlett Mall next to the town's frog pond and just a short distance from Route 1. This still active courthouse was built by famous Boston Architect Charles Bulfinch and opened to perform the business of the court in 1804. Many famous lawyers have argued cases in this building, including Daniel Webster and John Quincy Adams. One of its most well-known moments in history came in 1976, when a home-grown group of terrorists calling themselves the Fred Hampton Unit of the Peoples Front, placed a bomb inside the building, blowing out all the windows, severely damaging the northeast corner, and creating a huge hole in the floor. The bomb makers were eventually sent to prison and the building was repaired, but you can still see the patch in the northeast corner, a permanent reminder of an uneasy time in our history.

## THE NEWBURYPORT TURNPIKE

The Straight Road, as many have called it, was the brainchild of investors whose intention was to open a direct route from Newburyport to Boston. The idea was to build an "express" route that bypassed village and town centers, especially Salem, a very busy commercial port at that time. They wanted to create the shortest possible route to Boston. The road builders were given their instructions to "Build the road straight; south 24 degrees west and to follow that course as directly as possible to the Chelsea Bridge." The road was also supposed to be fairly level, not rising more than one foot in twenty, but anyone riding along the Topsfield section today knows that goal was way off the mark.

Soon after leaving Newburyport you enter a place known as the Great Marsh. This greenbelt of mudflats, marsh, barrier beaches, and tidal rivers is the largest salt marsh in New England, covering an area from Rockport on Cape Ann to New Hampshire. Farmers in the area have historically cut salt hay for use on the farm, and some still do today. Driving south on Route 1 in Newbury, if you look to the left as you come to the marsh, you can still see some classic hay staddles in the Great Salt Marsh.

**RIGHT:** The Great Marsh is part of the largest salt marsh in New England. Marshes are one of the richest ecosystems in the world and harbor an extensive and diverse collection of species. Salt marshes also protect the shore. Acting like a giant sponge, marshes absorb a great deal of destructive energy from storms that batter the coast. They also filter out contaminants that leach into waterways, threatening many important species in the food chain.

Kids enjoying the YOYO. One of the many rides at the Topsfield Fair.

**LEFT:** In its early days the fair moved around, but today the Topsfield Fair, the oldest fair in America, is permanently located in Topsfield, on the former Treadwell Farm.

# TOPSFIELD

## THE TOPSFIELD FAIR

The Topsfield Fair, held each year in October, is the oldest agricultural fair in the United States. In 1818, a group of farmers met in a local Topsfield tavern to form the Essex Agricultural Society, with the mission of educating farmers. The group held their first exhibition on October 5, 1820 and have been doing so for almost 200 years. The fair has been held every year, apart from six years—three during the Civil War and three during World War II.

Today the fair still holds to its core mission and hosts agricultural demonstrations and livestock events—the largest pumpkin contest is a fair favorite. It also has a very popular midway with rides, games, and food stands that contribute to its overall success.

**ABOVE:** Livestock is still an important part of the fair and is judged annually. **LEFT:** The author's daughter holds a baby chick born at the fair.

# DANVERS

As a rural farming community, Danvers, once nicknamed Onion Town, is famous for the development of the Danvers Half Long Carrot and the Danvers Onion (still available from seed companies today). It's also known for one of the more sinister events in colonial history— the Salem Witchcraft Trials. Salem will be forever connected to the witch trials of 1692 but "Salem Village," where many of the "afflicted" girls lived, is actually present-day Danvers, and was the epicenter of the hunt.

When the hysteria finally came to an end, more than 150 people had been accused of being witches, with twenty being put to death, one pressed, and the other nineteen hanged.

## PUTNAM PANTRY

The Putnam name has been synonymous with Danvers since the area was settled in 1636, and this establishment has been selling candy and make-your-own ice-cream sundaes since 1951,

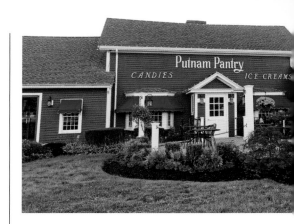

when the Putnams converted an old shoe manufacturing shop into the Pantry. Today you can still buy a box of their hand-made chocolates.

Behind the Pantry is a nondescript white clapboard house. It's the birthplace of General Israel Putman, a veteran of the French and Indian War and the America's Revolution. The original section of the house was built in 1648, and was home to twelve generations of Putnams. Joseph Putnam, Israel's father, lived in the house during the witchcraft hysteria of the 1690s and made it known that anyone coming

to his home to accuse members of his family of witchcraft—his sister-in-law and niece both claimed to be "afflicted"—would be met with loaded guns. No one ever came, and none of his family was ever accused of witchcraft, lending credence to the belief that the accusations of 1692 were more about settling debts than rooting out evil.

## THE SAUGUS STRIP

This section of Route 1 is the economic artery that feeds Boston's North Shore and for the mile-long stretch through the city of Saugus the highway is a Disneyland of family restaurants—iconic marvels like the Ship Restaurant, with its life-size red schooner appended to a make-believe New England village; Prince's

Restaurant, a pizza palace with a reproduction of the Leaning Tower of Pisa; the giant faux-timbered Continental; and the formidable Kowloon, featuring a grass-hut motif and snarling Polynesian totems.

## THE SHIP

Just down the road is a place called Ship Haven, more commonly known as "The Ship," a local restaurant with a unique layout that stands out among the rest of the eateries along this section of Route 1. In 1933, after many years at sea, Captain James Wilkinson of Gloucester opened a small food stand on the side of the road in Lynnfield. His true love, however, still rested with the sea and he yearned to stand on the deck of a ship again. So he built one. Captain Wilkinson's ship sits on the site of his old food stand and is today part of the Christmas Tree Shop complex.

## THE LEANING TOWER OF PIZZA

The actual name is Prince Pizzeria but is better known around the North Shore as "The Leaning Tower of Pizza". Owned by the Castraberti family, it's billed as the largest family-owned pizzeria in America. That may be true but it wasn't always the case. In the late 1950s, it was a twelve-seat pizza shop owned by the Prince Macaroni Company of Lowell. The business was in debt and slowly

**ABOVE:** Prince's Pizza in Saugus, one of a number of eclectic eateries along this section of Route 1.

closing down until Prince employee Arthur Castraberti agreed to take over management of the tiny Saugus pizza shop, with the goal of paying off the debt, showing a profit, and eventually owning it. It has been in his family ever since.

## BIG CACTUS

Any stranger driving through Saugus will undoubtedly wonder what the deal is with the giant cactus sitting at the side of the road. For forty years the Hilltop Steakhouse with its plastic cows and giant cactus, sat on the southbound side of Route 1, serving up prime steak dinners to thousands of customers in one of its western themed dining rooms. At the height of its popularity, it was satisfying more than

seven-thousand customers a day. The restaurant was the brain child of Frank Giuffrida, and the cactus was erected in homage to his favorite film star, John Wayne.

Today the restaurant is gone, the plastic cows are "grazing" at a local shopping mall, and the only evidence that something existed here is the sixty-eight foot cactus.

Frank Giuffrida's giant cactus, one part of the famous Hilltop Steakhouse, waits on the side of the road for a new development.

# BOSTON

The view from the Boston side of the Tobin Bridge is an inspiring tableau of a historic city still vibrant and full of life. On the right-hand side is the Bunker Hill Monument, a granite monolith rising out of Boston's old Charlestown neighborhood.

The monument is actually located on Breed's Hill, where most of the fighting occurred during the battle. On a foggy night in June 16, 1775, Washington's militia moved forward to fortify Bunker Hill, mistakenly digging in on Breed's Hill, placing them closer to Boston. This made them a bigger threat to the British, who attacked the next morning. The British won the battle but at the extreme cost of over 1,000 casualties. Although victorious, it was the beginning of the end for the British occupation of Boston.

Statue of Colonel William Prescott in front of the Bunker Hill Monument.

Bunker Hill Monument located on Breed's Hill in Boston's Charlestown neighborhood

At the base of Breed's Hill in the shadow of the Bunker Hill Monument, is a small open-space known as City Square Park. The park was once the site of the Three-Cranes Tavern in the fledgling community of Charlestown until one day in June of 1775, when British troops, frustrated during the Battle of Bunker Hill, burned most of it to the ground.

It wasn't until the second half of the twentieth century, when the City of Boston began exploring in preparation for the Big Dig project, that archeologists discovered remains of John Winthrop's Great House.

In 1629, John Winthrop, the man usually recognized as the founder of Boston, lead a group of settlers in search of a new site to build a community. The first building constructed was the Great House. It was a temporary structure used by Winthrop as housing and to conduct business.

The Three Cranes Tavern was eventually built on the site and foundation of the Great House, lost to history until its discovery over three-hundred years later.

**TOP:** The site of Boston's historic Three-Cranes Tavern and John Winthrop's Great House. **ABOVE:** City Square Park in Boston's Charlestown neighborhood. In 1628, Governor John Winthrop built his Great House on this site. A year later Winthrop moved the colony to what is known today as Beacon Hill.

## THE CHARLESTOWN NAVY YARD

The Charlestown Navy Yard is located on the left-hand side of the Tobin Bridge, near the Route 1 off-ramps. The yard is one of the oldest in the Nation and from 1800 until its closing in 1974 it built over 200 naval ships. Today it's home to the USS *Constitution* (Old Ironsides), the oldest active naval ship in the world; the USS *Cassin Young*, a World War II destroyer that fought with distinction in the Pacific; the Constitution Museum; and Boston National Historic Park.

## THE UNION OYSTER HOUSE

Located on Union Street next to the Rose Kennedy Greenway, the Union Oyster House, with its famous semi-circular oyster bar has been serving customers since 1826. One of the oldest restaurants in Boston, it has a storied past and has been visited by the likes of Daniel Webster, John Adams, John Hancock, and John F. Kennedy. Daniel Webster liked to stand at the oyster bar while JFK preferred one of the upstairs booths.

**ABOVE:** This is the site of the Boston Tea Party. On the night of December 16, 1773, members of the Son's of Liberty dressed as Indians boarded three ships (the *Eleonor,* a merchant ship and the *Beaver* and the *Dartmouth,* both whaling ships) and proceeded to dump 340 chests of East India Company tea into Boston Harbor in protest of the Tea Act of 1773.

The three-story brick building that houses this timeless treasure was also home to quite a bit of activity during the Revolution. Union Street, laid out in 1636, is one of the oldest streets in Boston and when the building was originally built in 1742 the wharfs of Boston's waterfront came right up to the back door. *The Massachusetts Spy*, the oldest newspaper in America, was printed upstairs in the 1700s; and in 1796, Louis Phillippe, future king of France, lived in an apartment on the second floor. In 1826 the building became a restaurant known as the Atwood & Bacon, with its now famous circular oyster bar serving seafood such as Virginia Oysters and Ipswich clams.

**ABOVE RIGHT:** The Union Oyster House began serving food in 1826 and is considered the oldest restaurant in America. The pre-Revolutionary War building was constructed next to harbor wharfs before the advent of land reclamation. Today it sits close to Route 1, which runs underground through much of downtown Boston.

## THE BELL IN HAND TAVERN

The Bell in Hand Tavern opened in 1795 and is one of the oldest taverns in Boston. The original owner was a man named Jimmy Wilson, Boston's town crier for over fifty years. Great food, good music, and a part of Boston and our nation's history, the tavern is a true original. The Bell in Hand has occupied its current site since 1844. It was originally located near Boston's Old City Hall which still houses one of the tavern's original signs.

## ROSE FITZGERALD KENNEDY GREENWAY

Today, Route 1 has been pushed underground and the swath of land in its place is known as the Rose Fitzgerald Kennedy Greenway. The Greenway is a series of parks running from Charlestown in the north to Chinatown in the south and has transformed the city landscape.

The Greenway abuts Quincy Market, the historic market next to Faneuil Hall. Faneuil Hall had outgrown its first floor market space by the time Boston had become a city in the early 1800s and Quincy Market was built to accommodate additional vendors. The market functioned as a meat and produce supply market until the early 1970s, when the complex was redeveloped as a restaurant, food stall, and merchandise marketplace. Today

Part of the Rose Kennedy Greenway, the Circle of Animals is a favorite with kid's.

it's one of the most visited tourist attractions in America. On Fridays and Saturdays produce vendors and fish mongers line the streets and are open for business in the Haymarket area and along Blackstone Street. This historic outdoor market has been in business since 1830.

## THE BOSTON ROWING CENTER

The Boston Rowing Center is located under a bridge in the Fort Point Channel, not far from Route 1. The program is run by the Hull Lifesaving Museum, whose goal is to teach rowing

**LEFT:** Quincy Market in the fall. **ABOVE:** The Boston Rowing Center.

and boat safety, while providing safe, affordable access to Boston Harbor. Classes are open to all, and they have programs for varying levels of competence. They can be found behind the Barking Crab restaurant at 88 Sleeper Street.

## SOUTHEAST EXPRESSWAY GAS TANK

The Dorchester Gas Tank is visible along Route 1 with its bold swatches that seemingly splash over the sides of the tank in a rainbow of colors. This gigantic display is one of the largest copyrighted art pieces in the world and is the creation of Corita Kent, a one-time Catholic nun and Vietnam War protester. When Kent created the piece in 1971 it immediately became controversial because it seemed to display the profile of Ho Chi Minh, the North Vietnamese leader, in its blue stripe. In 1992 the original painted tank was demolished and the artwork was reproduced on an adjacent tank, much to the dismay of many veterans groups. There were others who complained as well, feeling that Ho's features were intentionally softened in the new version.

## HISTORIC SITES

**Boston National Historic Park**

**Bunker Hill Monument**

**Bunker Hill Museum Faneuil Hall Visitor Center**

**Charlestown Navy Yard**

**Charlestown Navy Yard Visitor Center**

**Faneuil Hall, The Great Hall**

**USS *Constitution***

**USS *Constitution* Museum**

**LEFT:** The Southeast Expressway Gas Tank.

# FOXBOROUGH

## PATRIOT PLACE

It's not unusual to see 25,000 fans show up for a pre-season practice. The New England Patriots have become one of the premier football teams in the country, and their facility has kept pace with their success. Foxborough was once home to Schaefer Stadium, a cold, damp, windy concrete box, known more for its lack of amenities than for its sports team, but all that changed in 2002 when a new stadium, under new ownership, opened on the site of the old field's parking lot. The 68,000-seat stadium also includes 6,000 luxury seats and 82 luxury suites, a shopping mall, restaurants, hotel, movie theatres, museum, even a cranberry bog and nature trails. The team has sold out every pre-season, regular season, and playoff game since moving into the new facility in 2002.

**LEFT:** Patriot Place is home to the New England Patriots football team and the New England Revolution soccer team, but its more than just a sports destination. Patriot's Place has it all, including an open-air shopping center, lodging, and restaurants. And it's home to The Nature Trail, a half-mile trail that includes a 32-acre cranberry wetland.

Slater's Mill is located on the banks of the Seekonk River and is heralded as the location of the Industrial Revolution in America.

# RHODE ISLAND

Pawtucket • Providence • Cranston • Warwick • East Greenwich • North Kingstown • South Kingstown • Narragansett • Charlestown • Westerly

>>>It's easy to pass over Rhode Island. It's the smallest state in the nation at only 37 miles wide and 48 miles long, but the Ocean State has 400 miles of shoreline and Route 1 runs along the Lower Post Road for over 50 miles of beautiful shore views.

If you choose to slow down a little, Rhode Island can feel like a trip back in time. It's the birthplace of Narragansett Beer, the beer of the Red Sox of my childhood. "Hi Neighbor . . . Have a 'Gansett" still rings in my ears, from the radio broadcasts of my youth. Rhode Island is also the home of Coffee Milk, Del's Frozen Lemonade, the Big Blue Bug, and Allies Donuts. It's the birthplace of the industrial revolution and the classic American diner.

## PAWTUCKET

Slater Mill sits just across the way from Route 1 on the banks of the Seekonk River in Pawtucket. Often described as the first cotton mill in America, it's heralded by many as the birthplace of the Industrial Revolution. Slater Mill harnessed water power to run its operation and refined some of the industrial techniques previously smuggled to the colonies from Britain and used in Massachusetts at the turn of the eighteenth century.

The Slater Mill site consists of three historic buildings: the mill, a wood structure that was powered by water; Wilkinson's Mill, a stone building that was steam powered; and the Sylvanus Brown House.

## MODERN DINER

It's generally accepted that the idea of the diner, or "canteen," started in Rhode Island when a man named Walter Scott began selling food from a horse-drawn carriage on the streets of Providence.

The Modern Diner on East Street in Pawtucket is a 1940 Sterling Streamliner built by the J.D. Judkins Company of Merrimac, Massachusetts. The Streamliners were designed to resembled the sleek trains of the time. Only nineteen were built and the Modern is one of only two remaining; the other is located in Salem. The bullet-nosed Modern has the distinction of being the first diner listed on the National Register of Historic Places, a feat that saved it from destruction in 1978, during an era of urban renewal in Pawtucket.

The Modern's menu has all of the basic diner fair, as well as up to thirty specials that are posted daily. Two things I love about this place is their linguica and their famous dish, the Jimmie Gimmie—two poached eggs on an English muffin with sliced tomatoes, melted cheese, and bacon.

**ABOVE:** Pawtucket's Modern Diner a classic 1940s Sterling Streamliner built in Merrimac, Massachusetts and designed to look like a train engine.

# PROVIDENCE

## THE NORTH BURIAL GROUND

Travelling south on Route 1 in Providence will bring you to the North Burial Ground, a 110-acre cemetery established in 1700.

Many cemeteries during this era were laid out using an English landscape garden design with park benches, exotic trees, large flower beds, and wandering pathways. For many, these open spaces were viewed as a rural sanctuary in an area of increasing urban and industrial sprawl.

Two writers on the cutting edge of the horror genre, Edgar Allen Poe in the nineteenth century and H. P. Lovecraft in the twentieth, will be forever associated with Providence's North Burial Ground and College Hill neighborhood, particularly Benefit Street.

**RIGHT:** Providence's first cemetery, the North Burial Ground.

The Sarah Helen Whitman house located on Benefit Street in Providence.

While walking with a friend, Edgar Allen Poe noticed a woman in her rose garden at 88 Benefit Street. The woman was Sarah Helen Whitman, a transcendentalist with an interest in science and the occult, often holding séances in her home with friends, attempting to talk to the dead. Although Poe didn't know it at the time, she was a fan of his writing. Shortly after they began courting.

Poe was a troubled man who drank too much and dabbled in drugs. Helen finally agreed to marry Poe, but only if he gave up drinking. Poe agreed, but lapsed a few days later. When Sarah found out, she cut off the engagement.

Within a year, Edgar Allen Poe was found wandering the streets of Baltimore, incoherent and "out of his mind." He died in the hospital four days later on October 7, 1849.

Sarah died in 1878 and is buried in Providence's North Burial Ground, the same place she once took long walks with Poe. The house at 88 Benefit Street is much the same today as when Poe came upon Sarah in her garden. The rose garden is still behind the house, just one street over from Route 1.

Howard Phillips Lovecraft was born in Providence and although he received recognition for his writing later in life, he died almost penniless in 1937 at the age of thirty-six. He made a frugal living with his horror fiction, sometimes ghost writing for other writers. One of his stories, *The Shunned House*, takes place at 135 Benefit Street, his aunt's former home that was built on a family graveyard. Many of the houses on Benefit Street had family graves in their yards and most were moved when the street was widened. But Lovecraft's story details the few that were left behind at Number 135.

The Shunned House was supposed to be Lovecraft's first published book, but only 250 were printed (but were never bound). Eventually about fifty were bound and sold sometime after Lovecraft's death. Despite never hitting it big as a writer, today an original copy of *The Shunned House* sells for about $11,000.

**ABOVE:** *The Shunned House* story took place at this home on Benefit Street.

## RHODE ISLAND STATE HOUSE

The Rhode Island State House sits atop a hill at 82 Smith Street in Providence. The cornerstone was laid in 1895 and when it was completed, it became the state's seventh statehouse building. The exterior of the building has a strikingly white appearance owing to the Georgia marble used in its construction, and its massive dome is one of the largest self-supported marble domes in the world. The gilded statue, known as Independent Man, located on the top of the building, is a striking contrast to the marble exterior and symbolizes independence and tolerance, beliefs of Rhode Island's founder Roger Williams.

**LEFT:** Rhode Island's State House dome with "Independent Man" standing on top.

**ABOVE AND OPPOSITE:** Route 1 passes through East Greenwich, Rhode Island, a quintessential New England village on the Atlantic Ocean. It is home to restaurants, shops, bakeries, coffee shops, and restaurants, including Jigger's Diner, the Odeum Arts Center, and the one of a kind Greenwich Hotel. It also has a picturesque marina on Greenwich Bay and is home to Goddard Memorial State Park. The park is the most visited metropolitan park in the state and people come to enjoy its golf course, bridle paths, equestrian center, and performing arts complex.

## EAST GREENWICH

East Greenwich is a small town on Narragansett Bay with a rich history dating back to its incorporation in 1677. One of the stranger stories about this wonderful example of small town Rhode Island, is the Legend of *The Greenwich Voyager*. As the story goes, a Navy captain named Joseph Jonathan and his crew captured a group of extortionists trying to escape with a ransom in gold. The allure of more than 1,000 pounds of gold was too much of a temptation for the naval officer, and he stole the gold. Without the gold as evidence, the extortionists were released, only to be found dead along with Capt. Jonathan in his home . The gold was never found, buried someplace in the town, probably inside present day Goddard Memorial State Park. The story goes on to warn everyone that if the gold is ever removed, the town will crumble.

Today East Greenwich is home to a revitalized downtown, and Main Street (Route 1)

**RIGHT:** Jigger's Diner continues its tradition of selling some of the best diner food in town.

**OPPOSITE LEFT:** Quonset hut on the grounds of the Seabee Museum in Davisville. **OPPOSITE RIGHT:** The Fighting Seabee's statue on the grounds of the Seabee Museum in Davisville.

## EAT HERE

**Jiggers Diner**
**The Greenwich Hotel**
**The Greenwich Odeum**

is lined with all sorts of eclectic shops and restaurants. There's Jiggers Diner, a 1947 Worcester dining car serving some of the best food in town. The Greenwich Hotel, built in 1896, with its classic neon sign is a local bar and music establishment. Babe Ruth is rumored to have been a frequent visitor at the hotel. True or not, the Greenwich Hotel is a great place to relax and catch a few tunes—even the bar tender is a member of the band. The Odeum opened in 1926 as The Greenwich Theater, a vintage vaudeville house. It had its ups-and-downs but is open again and considered by many to be one of the best performing arts venues in Rhode Island.

# DAVISVILLE

## THE FIGHTING SEABEES

When most people hear the phrase The Fighting Seabees they usually think of the fictionalized 1944 movie starring John Wayne. However the real story of the Seabees—the Navy's Construction Battalions (CBs)—begins in Davisville, Rhode Island. Davisville is the original home of the Seabees and the Seabee Museum and Memorial Park located along Route 1 at 21 Iafrate Way in North Kingstown.

At the onset of World War II, the Navy realized it needed its own team to build naval bases around the globe. Until then, civilian contractors had done the work. In 1942, the base at Davisville became operational, and the Seabees were born. There motto is *Construimus, Batuimus* "We build. We Fight," with the adage of "We do the difficult immediately, the impossible takes a little longer."

The Navy's construction battalions have fought all over the world, and have been involved in every major conflict. They are prepared to fight, but they also do a lot of building for humanitarian purposes, especially during times of disaster.

## SMITH'S CASTLE

Smith's Castle is located at 55 Richard Smith Drive in the North Kingstown village of Wickford. The property was once the site of Roger Williams' trading post, built on land given to him by the Narraganset Indians. When Richard Smith bought the land and trading post from Williams he built a larger house that became known as Smith's Castle. In retaliation for his support of the militia during King Philip's War, the Narragansets burned down the original structure. Smith built the current "castle" in 1678. The property has a storied history, although not all of it is proud. The owners once held slaves who performed much of the work on the homestead. Designated a National Historic Landmark in 1993, it provides educational programming.

Smith's Castle in North Kingstown's Wickford Village.

The Gilbert Stuart Birthplace and Museum.

## GILBERT STUART BIRTHPLACE AND MUSEUM

Gilbert Stuart was considered by many to be the most recognized portraitist in America, owing largely to his unfinished portrait of George Washington, the same one that appeared on the one-dollar bill for over one hundred years, as well as numerous postage stamps.

Stewart was born in 1755 in Saunderstown Rhode Island, a village of North Kingstown.

His dad ran a snuff mill—the first snuff mill built in America, out of the family home, and today you can visit his birthplace, including the restored mill. Gilbert produced over 1,000 portraits, including the first five presidents of the United States.

The site was designated a National Historic Landmark in 1965.

# CHARLESTOWN

## THE FANTASTIC UMBRELLA FACTORY

**TOP:** The General Store at the Umbrella Factory Farm. **ABOVE:** The Umbrella Factory.

The Fantastic Umbrella Factory is located a short distance off Route 1 in Charlestown, Rhode Island. That section of Route 1 feels, looks, and acts like a modern-day highway with driving and passing lanes, a median strip, and breakdown lane. In contrast, entering the realm of the Umbrella Factory feels like porting back to the sixties. The site was once a farm, but today it's a group of shops sprinkled around the property interspersed with walkways, gardens, benches, and the occasional duck. There's a general store selling candy, charms, and tie-dyed items, as well as Small Axe Productions located in an old barn owned by a glass blower and a potter. There is a small animal farm, a stand selling eyeglass frames, a place called the Umbrella Factory Gardens, and a food stand. Visit and decide for yourself, but I'll stick to my original conclusion that this is where at least some of the old hippies landed.

Ninigret National Wildlife Refuge was established in 1970, but before that the land was home to the Naval Auxiliary Air Station Charlestown. During World War II the air station trained night fighter Pilots and pilots learning to fly the Hellcat, the primary World War II fighter used by the Navy. A young George H. W. Bush trained at Air Station Charlestown before shipping out to the South Pacific.

Today, a short segment of runway three-zero still exists at Ninigret. There's also a sign at the small section of runway three-zero that explains the following:

### "Charlietown"

*Look beneath your feet. You are standing on what was once Runway 30 of the Charlestown Naval Auxiliary Landing Field, or "Charlietown," as the young pilots called it.*

**RIGHT:** The old Naval Auxiliary Air Station Charlestown runway at the Ninigret National Wildlife Sanctuary. In 1942 this was a training station for U.S. Navy fighter pilots. George W. Bush, future President of the United States learned to fly the Hellcat fighter at NAAS Charlestown.

## NIGHT FIGHTER PILOTS

In 1942, in support of the air and sea missions of World War II, the Navy purchased the Hunter Harbor summer colony and nearly 600 acres of farmland along Ninigret Pond to create a landing and training field for night fighter pilots. These young pilots, ranging in age from 19 to 23, were trained to fly without lights and with minimal radio contact, relying entirely on their instruments. The dangers of using only primitive radar, combined with the hazardous weather conditions of the northeast, resulted in many flight accidents in and around Charlestown.

## FLYING A HELLCAT

Runway 30, one of three runways at the landing field, was named after the first two digits of the compass reading used by the pilots. Each runway was a minimum of 200 feet wide and 4,800 feet long, with the longest runway measuring 5,800 feet. The primary Naval fighter used during the war was the Hellcat. The base could hold aup to 300 of these planes at one time. There were two taxiways and over 150 buildings, including hangers, dining rooms, bunkers, enlisted and officer quarters, an administration building, a radio transmitter building, a wastewater treatment plant, and a fire station. Because training at the base began almost two years before the barracks were constructed, as many as 1,500 men lived in tents at nearby Burlingame State Park.

## BOUNCE DRILLS

Pilots trained for four months in Charlestown before heading out for duty in the South Pacific. Training consisted of 500 hours flight time and included tactics, gunnery, carrier landing, navigation, and instrument flying during the day and at night. For catapult training, a wooden carrier deck with a catapult was constructed adjacent to Runway 22. Neighboring children would watch from a distance as the novice pilots

The village of Wickford, part in North Kingstown.

landed on the simulated carrier deck. These training landings became known as "bounce drills," as the planes bounced onto the carrier.

## TRAINING A FUTURE PRESIDENT

As a young man, George H.W. Bush was stationed at Charlestown to learn to fly the TBM-1 Avenger, a big plane with a 50-foot wingspan. He named her "Barbara" after a young debutante he was dating. Barbara, of course, later became his wife and the First Lady.

## WESTERLY

Route 1's last stop in Rhode Island is the historic town of Westerly. The town sits on the eastern bank of the Pawcatuck River, just across a small bridge from Pawcatuck, Connecticut. The town seal carries the image of three salmon, memorializing the fish that once swam six miles upriver during its spring migration from the Atlantic Ocean.

Downtown Westerly is part of a historic district including over fifty structures. Its compact urban core includes many architectural styles, making it one of the "most intact, small-town downtowns" in Rhode Island. The McCormick Department Store, located at the head of Dixon Square is a good example of

**ABOVE LEFT:** The Pawcatuck River and the bridge that crosses the border between Westerly, Rhode Island and Stonington, Connecticut. **ABOVE:** Downtown Westerly.

**Allie's Donuts**
Ranked best donut shop in Rhode Island.

**Mill's Tavern**
Recognized by TripExperts with two Experts'
Choice Award.

**Oak Hill Tavern and Barbeque**
Once a Stagecoach stop The Oak Hill Tavern meta-
morphosed into a casual Restaurant/Tavern open
seven days a week featuring BBQ Ribs & Chicken,
Steaks, Seafood, Burgers & more.

**The Modern Diner**
Home to Classic comfort foods and weekend breakfast specials at this historic train car eatery.

late Victorian design; and just across the street, looming high above most of the other buildings, is the early twentieth-century Washington Trust Building. Washington Trust is the oldest community bank in the nation. Even the scuppers that accept rainwater from the roof are in the shape of bank vaults.

# CONNECTICUT

Stonington ● Mystic ● Groton ● New London ● Waterford ● East Lyme ● Old Lyme ● Old Saybrook ●
Westbrook ● Clinton ● Madison ● Guilford ● Branford ● East Haven ● New Haven ● West Haven ●
Orange ● Milford ● Stratford ● Bridgeport ● Fairfield ● Westport–Norwalk ● Darien ● Stamford ● Greenwich

〉〉〉〉In Connecticut, Route 1 hugs the shoreline as it travels 117 miles through small hamlets and town centers, as well as larger cities like New Haven. One of the original thirteen colonies, Connecticut also has the distinction of being the home of many other originals. The Frisbee was invented in Bridgeport, the first free public library was opened in Salisbury, and the first amusement park was built in Bristol. Other firsts include the first submarine, pay phone, hamburger, and dictionary.

## MYSTIC

Route 1 brushes past Stonington on its way to the village of Mystic, home to historic Mystic Seaport.

The Seaport was established in 1929 on the site of a former shipyard with the mission of preserving America's maritime history. Today it encompasses nineteen acres of land on the Mystic River and is the premier maritime history museum in the country. The centerpiece is the whaleship, *Charles W. Morgan*.

In addition to the *Morgan*, the museum boasts over 500 historic vessels, including the *L.A. Dutton*, a grand banks fishing schooner built in Essex Massachusetts, and the 60-foot *Roann*, an "eastern rigged" dragger with its working deck forward and pilothouse aft. Draggers like the *Roann* used nets and "doors" to

**ABOVE:** Historic drawbridge over the Mystic River in Stonington. **RIGHT:** Historic shop buildings of Mystic Village.

drag for fish along the bottom as opposed to the hooks and lines used by the older fishing schooners.

## MYSTIC PIZZA

Mystic Pizza opened in 1973, and was just another pizza joint along the shoreline of Connecticut until screenwriter Amy Jones, who was vacationing in the area, happened to walk in. She decided to make the small pizzeria the focal point of a new movie, released as *Mystic Pizza* in 1988. A coming of age movie centered around three women working as waitresses, it was a break-out movie for Julia Roberts and Matt Damon's first movie role. Go in and have a slice, if you're in the area, and maybe rent the movie when you get home.

## JOHN KELLEY STATUE

There's a small park at the corner of West Main and Bank Street in Mystic, with a statue of a man running accompanied by a dog. The statue and park pays homage to John Kelley, longtime runner, two-time Olympian, and winner of the 1957 Boston Marathon. For most people who knew him, the statue is also a memorial to the John Kelley they knew as a teacher, coach, writer, and friend. John taught at the Fitch School in Groton where he also coached cross-country track. He was a role model

**ABOVE:** Mystic Pizza Shop

**ABOVE:** Statue of John Kelley, winner of the Boston Marathon and longtime resident of Mystic, seen here with his dog Brutus, John's longtime running companion.

to many of his students, demonstrating the ideals of perseverance, strength, humility, and determination. John was a life-long resident of Mystic and often trained on the town's hills, making this small park the perfect location to honor him—and his frequent running companion, his dog Brutus.

# GROTON

## THE *NAUTILUS*

**ABOVE:** USS *Nautilus*, the first nuclear powered submarine and the first to reach the North Pole.

**OPPOSITE:** The Submarine Memorial in Groton honors those who served in the submarine corps.

Groton, framed by the Thames and Mystic Rivers, is steeped in maritime history, especially when it comes to the evolution of the submarine. David Bushnell, a student at Yale designed and built the first submarine in Old Saybrook in 1775, a one-man submersible, capable of running underwater with the potential to mine ships with explosives. A replica of the original can be seen at the Submarine Force Library and Museum located on the Thames River in Groton.

The Electric Boat Division of General Dynamics, founded in 1899, is in Groton and has been building submarines for the United States Navy for over 100 years.

## WORLD WAR II SUBMARINE MEMORIAL

The World War II Submarine Memorial is located on Bridge Street in Groton, between the intersections of Fairview Avenue and Thames Street. It is dedicated to the 52 submarines and the 3,617 submariners lost at sea during World War II. The memorial includes the conning tower of the USS *Flasher*. The *Flasher* was built by Electric Boat in Groton and was one of the most successful submarines to serve during the war. The memorial also includes a granite wall acknowledging each submarine lost, and a wall of honor with the names of the submariners lost at sea.

## SUBMARINE FORCE LIBRARY AND MUSEUM

The museum is operated by the Navy and traces submarine history from its beginning during the Revolutionary War to today's nuclear fleet. The highlight of a visit is a tour of the USS *Nautilus*, the Navy's first nuclear submarine. The tour allows visitors to experience the cramped living space that submariners still experience today.

The *Nautilus* was built and commissioned in 1951. She was the first submarine to reach the North Pole, crossing under the polar ice from the Pacific Ocean near Alaska and exiting near Greenland in the Atlantic. In 1957 she matched the accomplishments of Jules Verne's fictional namesake by logging over 60,000 nautical miles (20,000 leagues) under the sea.

There's one more historic site worth visiting before rejoining Route 1 and crossing the Thames River. Fort Griswold is a Revolutionary War fort built to defend Groton from the British. It is a traditional earthen fortification and was under the command of Colonel William Ledyard when it was attacked by the British in 1781. Along with Fort Trumbull on the western shore of the Thames, the Americans maintained a formidable position but the British had a secret weapon. Benedict Arnold, the American traitor, was in command of the British troops assaulting the forts. Arnold was born in Connecticut and had lived in Groton, and with his intimate knowledge of the fortifications, the British successfully captured both forts. The troops at Fort Griswold were massacred after surrendering, reportedly as retaliation for heavy British casualties. Arnold and his troops left Groton in flames.

Connecticut has made room for access to the shore with some of the biggest state parks in New England. Harkness Memorial, Rocky Neck, Hammonasset, Lighthouse Point, Sherwood Island, and Silver Sands are all large state parks allowing the public to enjoy one of the state's most precious natural resources.

### Harkness Memorial State Park, Waterford

The park is the former home and estate of the Harkness family. Located on Long Island Sound, the 230-acre former estate is home to a classical revival-style mansion, including a large garden complex and magnificent panoramic views of the sound. There are no swimming facilities at this site, but fishing, picnicking, and mansion tours are available.

### Rocky Neck State Park East, Lyme

This 6-acre park has a wide sandy beach and large stone pavilion and jetty. There is family camping available with wooded and open sites. Activities include saltwater fishing, swimming, bird watching, picnicking, and crabbing. Life guards are on duty during the summer. The park is open daily from 8 a.m. until sunset.

## EAT HERE

**Paul's Pasta Shop**
Pasta and sandwiches for lunch of dinner. Good food and very good service. They also have take-out available.

**Sea Swirl**
Seafood shack offering great take-out. Has outdoor dining and great views.

**ABOVE:** Rocky Neck State Park in East Lyme.

### Hammonasset Beach State Park, Madison

Hammonasset has more than two miles of coarse sandy beachfront and is Connecticut's largest shoreline park. The beaches are handicap accessible and activities include swimming, fishing, camping, boating, and biking. Lifeguards are on duty during the regular summer season. The park has a large camping facility with most sites located in large fields. The beach also has a large boardwalk and many bathroom facilities. This park is an ideal location for observing the late-summer migration of the monarch butterfly. The beach is open from 8 a.m. until sunset, but campers and anglers may enter the park during the evening.

### Lighthouse Point State Park, New Haven

The park is located on the eastern point of New Haven Harbor in East Haven and is home to a historic lighthouse and carousel. The beach is sandy and well-groomed and the rocky outcropping to the right of the main beach is a great place for fishing. There are lots of activities, including swimming, boating, and picnicking. This is another park that is in the flight line of the monarch butterfly. The antique carousel is available for functions and the lighthouse is open for tours. There are lifeguards on duty during the summer season. The park is open daily from 7 a.m. until sunset.

Lighthouse Point State Park in
New Haven.

**Sherwood Island State Park, Westport**

Sherwood Island is Connecticut's first state park and consists of 235 acres along Westport's shoreline. The park has a wide sandy beach and plenty of fields for sports, room for picnicking, and lots of open space along the shoreline for saltwater fishing. The park is also home to a wonderful nature center. The park is open from 8 a.m. until sunset and lifeguards are on duty during the summer season.

**Silver Sands State Park, Milford**

Silver Sands has a wide sandy beach and is the location of Charles Island, rumored home of Captain Kidd's treasure. The island is connected to the mainland by a tombolo that is covered by water at high tide. There is a boardwalk connecting the state beach to Milford's Walnut Beach Park. Activities include fishing, shell collecting, boating, crabbing, and treasure hunting. The park is open from 8 a.m. until sunset, but is accessible during the evening hours for fishing. Lifeguards are on duty during the summer season.

# OLD LYME

## FLORENCE GRISWOLD MUSEUM

Florence Griswold was from an affluent Old Lyme family. After falling on hard times, she turned her home into a boarding house for artists, creating what would become the Lyme Art Colony. In 1899, artists began arriving and a new school of landscape painting was born. When Childe Hassam arrived in 1903, the school transformed itself, becoming an important center for American Impressionist painting.

The Florence Griswold Museum is a great place to visit if you are a fan of American art. While there, you can also visit the garden and grounds. The museum is located on Route 1 at 96 Lyme Street in Old Lyme Connecticut.

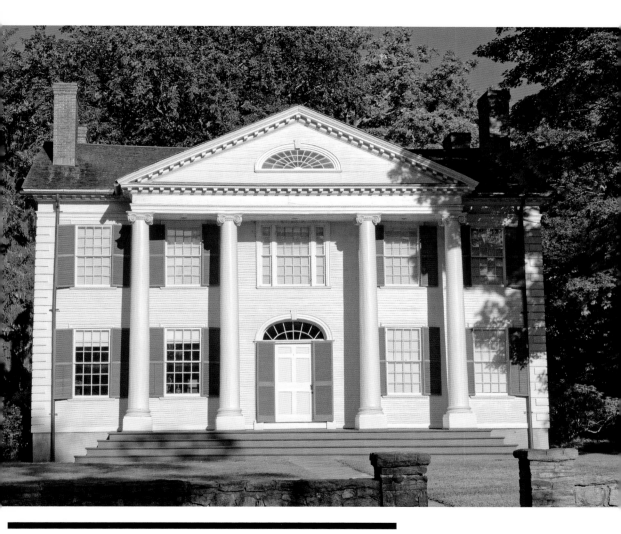

**ABOVE:** Florence Griswald Museum in Old Lyme, once home to the Lyme Art Colony and a focal point in the history of American Impressionist painting.

**ABOVE:** The East River in Gilford is one of hundreds of picturesque inlets scattered along coastal Connecticut. **RIGHT:** Route 1 through Madison.

# CONNECTICUT SHORE

The southern Connecticut shore is covered by large stretches of salt marsh, a protective barrier between land and ocean.

This part of the US-1 gives way to small stretches of undeveloped land interspersed with old homesteads and village centers. The town centers of Clinton, Madison, and Guilford are filled with antique shops, ice-cream parlors, and bakeries along Main Street, giving the feeling of stepping back in time.

For entertainment, there's the Madison Art Cinemas, which opened its doors in Madison in 1912. Today, it is a two-theatre operation but still has a hometown feel.

If you'd rather read a book, walk across the street to R.J. Julia Booksellers. It's been open for over 25 years and is one of the best independent bookstores in New England.

## BISHOP'S ORCHARD

The orchard was started by Walter Bishop in 1871, and seven generations later it's still going strong. Today, the farm is 300 acres, includes a winery and a 2,000-square-foot retail center. They also have a robust pick-your-own program that runs throughout the growing season. Their apple cider is excellent— they've been producing it since the 1930s, so they've had a lot of practice.

**ABOVE:** R.J. Julia Bookstore in Madison.

**ABOVE:** Bishop's Orchards in Gilford was started in 1871 and is seventh generation owned and operated. The Bishop families have had their roots in Guilford since 1639.

## THE PLACE RESTAURANT

In 1971, Gary and Vaughn Knowles bought a clambake business known as Whitey's off an old timer who'd been running clambakes by the side of the road since the 1940s. The brothers named the restaurant after Whitey's favorite phrase: *"There's no place, quite like this place, anywhere near this place, so this must be The Place."* And what a place it is. It's an outdoor seafood restaurant with little fanfare, taking the idea of eating in the rough to new dimensions. The simple round tables sit on tree stumps and stumps also serve as chairs. Roasted clams are the specialty, but they also serve lobster, fish, steak, chicken, and mussels. They even allow their customers to gussy up the place, if they'd like. You can bring your own tablecloths, candles, side dishes, and favorite alcoholic beverages.

**ABOVE:** Bill Miller's Castle in Branford.

## BILL MILLER'S CASTLE

In Branford there's an eye catcher of a building. It's Bill Miller's Castle. Bill had a vision of creating a castle out of an old horse barn and in 1965 that's exactly what he did. Today it's a popular location for weddings and other social functions, but Bill also offers the public a chance

ABOVE: Louis Lunch in New Haven.

to visit his unique and extravagant establishment. Just make reservations at one of the castle's special events. They serve brunch on Easter, Mother's Day, and Thanksgiving, and serve a special dinner on Valentine's Day. The cathedral ceilings, ornate stained-glass windows, and crystal chandeliers, along with the numerous fieldstone fireplaces, make any of these occasions a time to remember.

## NEW HAVEN

Route 1 traverses East Haven, New Haven, and West Haven, at times twisting through industrial sections of the waterfront, such as the oil storage district just before Milford. From East Haven to Fairfield, US-1 passes through dense commercial and urbanized neighborhoods packed with stop lights and stop-and-go traffic at times trying the patience of the traveler.

### LOUIS LUNCH

Louis Lunch, located on Crown Street in New Haven, holds claim to inventing the hamburger. Inventing might not be the correct word, but you know what I mean. Louis Lunch boasts that they served it first but whatever the actual story, Louis' is a pretty good one. In 1900 a customer in a hurry asked Louis if he could figure out how to make it "to go." He was in a hurry and couldn't wait, so Louis just stuck the paddy between two pieces of bread, sent him on his way, and the hamburger was born. Louis makes their patties using five different types of meat that they grind daily and cook on special grilles—the same grilles Louis bought in 1898.

Today the restaurant is run by Louis' great grandson, Jeff Lassen, and the philosophy at Louis is still the same: If it was good enough for 1900, it's good enough for today. So if you're lucky enough to make it to Louis Lunch, your hamburger will be served with bread—hamburger rolls didn't exist back in the day—and you'll also be limited in what you can get on your burger. The only toppings available are cheese, tomatoes, and onions. Yes, you guessed it. If it was good enough then, it's good enough now.

**ABOVE:** The PEZ Vistors Center in Orange offers over 4,000 square feet of all things PEZ.

## PEZ CANDY

Near New Haven, Orange is the home of Pez Candy. The company originated in Austria and has been around for over 80 years, satisfying the sweet tooths of children and adults with its unique candy. If you decide to stop and visit nobody will be disappointed. A tour lets you watch the candy being made and the gift shop is filled with new and old models of Pez dispensers available for purchase. There are also some interesting displays of older models and collectibles.

# NORWALK

## SWANKY FRANKS

Swanky Franks is a classic hotdog joint with the added appeal of being one-of-a-kind. There's nothing chain store about this place. Some people have called it a "greasy spoon," but they say it as a compliment, a term of endearment. The food at Swanky Franks is great, the service is too, and they make terrific shakes. This is the place to stop in Norwalk if you're looking for classic road food.

**EAT HERE**

**Bishop's Orchard**

**Louis' Lunch**

**PEZ Candy**

**The Place Restaurant**

**Stew Leonard's**

**Swanky Franks**

**LEFT:** Swanky Frank's in Norwalk is a classic hot dog stand. If you love hotdogs this is a nostolgic haven that shouldn't be missed.

**ABOVE AND ABOVE RIGHT:** Charles Leo Leonard, Stew's dad started the Clover Farms Dairy in Norwalk, Connecticut. The milk was delivered to the customer's door in trucks with plastic cows that mooed to kids in the neighborhood, helping the kids, and hopefully their parents, remember the brand. Stew brought the business a step further when he opened his dairy stores, considered by Ripley's Believe It or Not, to be the largest dairy store in the world.

## STEW LEONARD'S

When you drive into the parking lot at Stew Leonard's in Norwalk you pass a yellow milk delivery truck with a cow's head on the front. This was a creation of Stew's father when he ran a dairy farm and residential milk delivery was common practice.

Some of that showmanship must have rubbed off on Stew because his idea of unique entertainment has made Stew Leonard's Dairy Store the largest dairy store in the world. Going to Stew's is more like visiting an amusement park inside a grocery store.

The store is set up like a giant track. You begin at the starting line and end with the registers at the finish line. The store has a collection of animatronics for the customers' viewing pleasure—dancing milk cartons anyone? The store also prepares lots of in-store products, roasting their own coffee beans, making

Bridge over the Saugatuck River in Wesport with the Kings
Highway North Historic District in the background.

cheese, and popping popcorn. Besides the store itself, Stew's also has an ice-cream stand, garden center, petting zoo, and hamburger stand.

## GREENWICH

Trying to find the real coastal Connecticut can have you chasing your tail, and no part of the coast is harder to get a handle on than the Gold Coast from Westport to Greenwich. This is the place where the landscape begins to change as you get closer to the New York border. Westport, on the banks of the Saugatuck River, is considered the tenth wealthiest town in America of comparable size. The Kings Highway North Historic District is in Westport on the western shore of the river. On the eastern side is the shopping district, a small-town shopping district with chic New York-type fashion stores like Dovecote, Restoration Hardware, and Tiffany's.

The last town on Route 1 in Connecticut is Greenwich, considered by many to be one of

**ABOVE:** Historic Greenwich Ave. in Greewich.

the most affluent towns in New England, and a bedroom community for New York City. Much less of a tourist destination than other places along Route 1, Greenwich is home to hedge fund managers, bankers, and commuters lucky enough to live outside the Big Apple.

For those who find this the end of their Route 1 New England journey and want to head back to Fort Kent, make sure you go around the rotary after crossing the small bridge spanning the Byram River.

# ACKNOWLEDGMENTS

>>>>I want to thank my kids Jared and Caitie, now mature young adults, who traveled much of Route 1 with me when they were growing up; their mom Anne Marie, who helped me coordinate my crazy schedule of never-ending road trips; my grandfather, a farmer at heart who took me as a child on his annual pilgrimages to the Topsfield Fair; my parents, who introduced me to camping at Camden Hills State Park; my editors, Mike Steere and Stephanie Scott; my traveling companion, fellow photographer and "roadmaster" Eric Alexander, who logged countless hours of travel from the Canadian border to the New York state line; Eric's son, Ian, a budding photographer in his own right; and all my friends who over the years have traveled this majestic roadway, exploring it's history and wonders. Old friends like Ed and Linda Solomon; my old-school Outdoor Education teammates Brad Currier and Rhonda Fraser; my new/old friend and fellow curmudgeon Burt Carey; and all those unique individuals I met along the way that made project a memorable and special experience.